A NEW OWNER'S
GUIDE TO
GERMAN SHORTHAIRED POINTERS

JG-122

Overleaf: A German Shorthaired Pointer adult and puppy photographed by Isabelle Francais.

Opposite Page: Ch. Tabor's Don't Think Twice, owned by Joan Tabor.

The publisher wishes to acknowledge the following owners of the dogs in this book: Karen L. Allen, Toni Boyd, Michelle Burns, Julia Carroll, F. Del Prete, George and Karen Heaney, Paula Jones, Dot Kern, Sandra Kretz, Bruce and Ellen Ladenheim, Ken and Judy Marden, Iris and Ray Mones, M. Oakley, Pine Hill German Shorthaired Pointers, Dino and Doreen Russo, Joan and Joel Tabor, and Christine and Ken Tucker.

Photographers: Karen L. Allen, Michelle Burns, Isabelle Francais, Dot Kern, Sandra Kretz, Bruce and Ellen Ladenheim, Ken and Judy Marden, Mikron Photos, Ltd., Lynn Miller Photo-Graphics, Vince Serbin, M. Sisson, Louise Shattuck, and Joan and Joel Tabor.

The author acknowledges the contribution of Judy Iby to the following chapters: Health Care, Sport of Purebred Dogs, Identification and Finding the Lost Dog, Traveling with Your Dog, and Behavior and Canine Communication.

© by T.F.H. Publications, Inc.

Distributed in the UNITED STATES to the Pet Trade by T.F.H. Publications, Inc., One T.F.H. Plaza, Neptune City, NJ 07753; on the Internet at www.tfh.com; in CANADA Rolf C. Hagen Inc., 3225 Sartelon St. Laurent-Montreal Quebec H4R 1E8; Pet Trade by H & L Pet Supplies Inc., 27 Kingston Crescent, Kitchener, Ontario N2B 2T6; in ENGLAND by T.F.H. Publications, PO Box 15, Waterlooville PO7 6BQ; in AUSTRALIA AND THE SOUTH PACIFIC by T.F.H. (Australia), Pty. Ltd., Box 149, Brookvale 2100 N.S.W., Australia; in NEW ZEALAND by Brooklands Aquarium Ltd. 5 McGiven Drive, New Plymouth, RD1 New Zealand; in SOUTH AFRICA, Rolf C. Hagen S.A. (PTY.) LTD. P.O. Box 201199, Durban North 4016, South Africa; in JAPAN by T.F.H. Publications, Japan—Jiro Tsuda, 10-12-3 Ohjidai, Sakura, Chiba 285, Japan. Published by T.F.H. Publications, Inc.

MANUFACTURED IN THE
UNITED STATES OF AMERICA
BY T.F.H. PUBLICATIONS, INC.

A New Owner's Guide to
GERMAN SHORTHAIRED POINTERS

Joan Tabor

Contents

The German Shorthaired Pointer is a natural hunter and excels at fieldwork.

German Shorthaired Pointer puppies should be bright-eyed and alert.

Tabor's Liberty and Justice doing what she does best—tracking.

The well-socialized German Shorthaired Pointer will share even his favorite ball!

A loving German Shorthaired Pointer makes the ideal family pet.

HISTORY and Origin of the German Shorthaired Pointer

The German Shorthaired Pointer was developed to meet the changing needs of the 18th and 19th century hunters in Great Britain and continental Europe. With the breakup of large estates after the French Revolution and the Napoleonic wars, hunting privileges, once reserved for the aristocracy, had become within reach of the middle class Europeans. These Europeans found their needs best met by owning one, all-purpose dog that would hunt, point, retrieve, and track.

The German Shorthaired Pointer was developed as a breed to meet the needs of the 18th and 19th century hunter.

The Europeans had an expression that a man who went hunting with three dogs had no dog. Their objective was to develop one dog that would be capable in every sphere. His scenting ability had to be such that he could locate and point game at a reasonable distance for a foot hunter. He had to demonstrate the willingness to retrieve fur or feather, on land or in water.

The dog would have to demonstrate courage and the capability to destroy predators, such as wild cats and foxes, and possess the ability to scent the trail of a wounded animal. He also would have to be of sound temperament to protect his home and family and accompany them on their hunting excursions. In other words, this hunting dog would have to be versatile.

It is believed that the Germans crossed the old Spanish Pointer with the Hounds of St. Hubert. The exact mix that eventually evolved into the German Shorthaired Pointer is not clearly defined, nor can it be

The courageous German Shorthaired Pointer is well known for his hunting abilities in the field. Ch. Tabor's Chocolate Decadence owned by Joan Tabor and Julia Carroll.

accurately determined. What is clear is that the German Shorthaired Pointer that we know today became a breed in the late 19th century.

Early photographs of German Shorthaired Pointers depict them as heavier and more "houndy" than modern day Shorthairs. In the 1870s, the Germans were deeply divided between those who insisted that the German Shorthaired Pointer resemble the "early German Pointer" with round ears and a Roman nose, indicating hound influence, and those who believed that performance was more important, favoring the English Pointer influence. Performance won out, enabling the Germans to turn to the English Pointer for their speed, agility, and wind-scenting, "high nose" ability. What resulted was a physically more attractive dog with longer legs and lighter build, sharing a much closer resemblance to the modern day German Shorthaired Pointer. Today, most acknowledge the German Shorthaired Pointer as the result of crossing the old Spanish Pointer, English Foxhound, German tracking hound, and English Pointer.

Having established what the German Shorthaired Pointer should look like, in 1939, the Kurzhaar (Shorthair) breeders of Germany established a working trial for the German Shorthair, naming it after their club founder and historian, Dr. Paul Kleeman. In Germany, the title of Kleeman-Sieger is still regarded as the highest honor a German Shorthaired Pointer can hold.

THE GERMAN SHORTHAIRED POINTER COMES TO THE USA

German Shorthaired Pointers found their way into the

The GSP is the end result of crossing the Spanish Pointer, English Foxhound, German tracking hound, and English Pointer.

8

United States as early as 1880. Although these early arrivals were unregistered, photographs document their existence. Dr. Charles R. Thornton of Missoula, Montana, is the person credited with establishing the breed in this country through the importation of Senta V. Hohenbruck from Austria in 1925. He was attracted to the breed after reading a magazine article featuring the prominent Hohenbruck strain from Austria. Senta V. Hohenbruck arrived in Missoula in whelp (pregnant). Her litter, born on July 4, 1925, was the first German Shorthaired Pointer litter whelped in the United States.

The German Shorthaired Pointer is a versatile animal— the perfect canine companion as well as hunter.

The German Shorthaired Pointer made his first appearance in the United States as early as 1880. Ch. Keystone Kisses owned by Michelle Burns and Toni Boyd.

Dr. Thornton was so impressed with the field ability of Senta and her pups that he imported at least a dozen more German Shorthair Pointers from Austria and Germany.

Another prominent breed pioneer, Joseph Burkhart, imported three German Shorthairs to the United States. Burkhart mated Bob v. Schwarenberg and Arta v. Hohereusch, two of his imports, to produce Ch. Fritz v. Schwarenberg. Fritz was sold to Jack Shattuck, Jr., and was successfully mated, beginning a prominent line that has become the foundation of many of the modern day American kennels.

The American Kennel Club gave official recognition to the breed in 1930. The first two show titles awarded to German Shorthaired Pointers by the American Kennel Club went to two dogs of Dr. Thornton's breeding.

The German Shorthaired Pointer Club of America, Inc. (the Parent Club) was formed in 1938, and listed among its charter members are Joseph Burkhart, and Jack Shattuck, Jr.

The American Kennel Club recognized the German Shorthaired Pointer in 1930. Ch. Tabor's Zephyr of Orion owned by Joan and Joel Tabor.

Breeders have dedicated themselves to the welfare and development of the GSP throughout the years.

The American Kennel Club assigned the Parent Club the task of defining the breed type by developing a written breed standard. It would be impossible to promote and improve the breed if it didn't first define what the breed should look like. In May, 1946, the breed standard, which had been adapted from the German standard, was approved. The Parent Club had forseen the potential need to improve the definition of the Standard for what was considered true type. The Amended Articles in 1945 established a means by which the breed standard could be revised from time to time. It also established uniform judging methods for both field trials and bench (conformation) shows. The discussion about what constitutes true breed type goes on to this day.

The Parent Club was the first organization with field trial competition for the breed, enabling German Shorthaired Pointers to work towards their field, show, and dual Championships. Soon, other regional clubs formed and provided additional opportunities for German Shorthairs.

Today the parent club, with over 2000 members, is dedicated to the welfare of the breed and sponsors numerous national events designed to bring out the Shorthair's natural abilities. Events include National Field Championships, a National Specialty Show, a National Obedience Trial and a National Hunting Test, as well as both National Field and Show Futurities.

The German Shorthaired Pointer should give the impression of power, athleticism, and intelligence.

Since 1964, the Parent Club has published yearbooks that include a listing of all new champions and title holders and their pedigrees. It also includes the award winners of the year, new dual champions, top producers, and, since 1980, it contains the dogs elected into the German Shorthaired Pointer Hall of Fame. Yearbooks also include information on regional member clubs that operate under the auspices of the Parent Club.

The German Shorthaired Pointer Club of America (GSPCA) began publishing a magazine in 1988 called *Shorthair* which is included in the annual membership fee, but the magazine is no longer published.

The parent club sponsors educational seminars, judging seminars, genetic surveys, and supports an active breed rescue group. Membership in the GSPCA includes individuals of diverse interests in field trials, conformation shows, obedience and tracking trials, breeding, hunting, therapy dogs, and those who simply love the breed and keep them as lifetime companions.

The German Shorthaired Pointer is at home either as a family member or field hunter.

12

CHARACTERISTICS of the German Shorthaired Pointer

PHYSICAL ATTRIBUTES

Although somewhat small in stature, the German Shorthaired Pointer should give the impression of power. This well-balanced and aristocratic dog should possess an athletic build and appear intelligent and animated. Males stand 23 to 25 inches tall, and weigh between 55 to 70 pounds. Females are 21 to 23 inches tall and weigh 55 to 60 pounds.

Their coloring may be any combination of liver and white, from the solid liver, and liver roan, liver or white ticked, to a mostly white. Although the color combinations of solid black and black and white are ineligible to compete in American Kennel Club bench shows, they are registerable and may compete in field trials, hunt tests, and obedience trials. They are recognized as acceptable German Shorthaired Pointer colors in most other parts of the world. The visibility of many imports has increased the popularity of the black coloration in this country. A dog with any area of black, red, orange, lemon, or tan—or a solid white dog—is listed as a breed disqualification, and may not be exhibited in the show ring or receive a show championship. A movement is presently underway to try to have the color black removed from the list of disqualifications.

Even as a puppy, the GSP should have the distinctive coat color that sets him apart from other breeds.

14

The German Shorthaired Pointer has a docked tail and generally has the dewclaws on his forelegs removed. These procedures are done when the pups are three days old. There are health and safety, as well as aesthetic, reasons for this. However, many German Shorthairs in this country have not had these procedures done, either due to preference on the part of the breeder or ignorance. Dogs with undocked tails are faulted in the show ring.

A full-grown GSP will weigh anywhere between 55 and 70 pounds, depending on sex.

The short, thick coat of the German Shorthaired with its thick, furry under-coat, provides the perfect protection from injury in heavy cover and from cold when working in water or in the field in cold weather. The ideal coat should also be tightly knit and water repellant. These coats will

The GSP's coat may consist of any combination of liver and white. Pebbles, Cindy, Zephyr, and Stinker are examples of the different markings of the breed.

shed, particularly during the change of seasons, and those allergic to dog dander may have some difficulty coping with this.

If your German Shorthaired Pointer has been well cared for, he should live an average of 12 years, although some have been known to live 16 or 17 years. This is a fairly long life expectancy for a dog of this size.

ROLE IN MODERN SOCIETY

Although not one of the top ten dogs according to the American Kennel Club, the German Shorthaired Pointer has maintained considerable popularity in rankings. They are among the top five most popular Sporting Breeds. In recent years, the breed was ranked at around number 30 for all-breed popularity, placing it within the top 25 percent.

The German Shorthaired Pointer makes a wonderful family companion and relates well to children.

The German Shorthaired Pointer posses field dog qualities that maintain his popularity as an all-around gun dog. His versatility, the very reason for his creation as a breed, continues to fuel its popularity. There are few dogs that can staunchly point a bird, track wounded animals, retrieve on land or water, and have pleasing conformation, endurance, and the intelligence needed to be a family companion and watchdog.

In addition to hunting companions, the German Shorthaired Pointer has demonstrated his competitiveness in the show ring, in field, obedience, and in agility trials, and his usefulness as a service dog. Police departments and United States Custom agents have benefitted from the keen scenting ability of the Shorthair. Some of these dogs are used for drug, bomb and arson detection, and in search and rescue.

PERSONALITY AND TEMPERAMENT

The disposition and intelligence of the German Shorthaired Pointer makes him an outstanding family companion. They are

Among the top five most popular sporting breeds, the German Shorthaired Pointer is an athletic all-around gun dog. FC, AFC Timberdoodle's Bee-Line owned by Dot Kern. gregarious, energetic dogs, admired for their temperament and trainability. The German Shorthair relates well to children, visitors, and other dogs. Typically, the German Shorthair is outgoing and fun-loving. He should not be aggressive. German Shorthairs display a tremendous willingness to please whether at home or in the field. However, their love of game makes them very distractable outdoors, and for that reason they are best kept in enclosed or safe areas, except when hunting. Obedience training will make the Shorthair a pleasure to own and more reliable when on hunting excursions or other outings.

The German Shorthair is adaptable to most living situations, provided he has been given ample opportunity to exercise and has been kept in top physical condition. Younger dogs retain an effervescence which some people may find difficult to live with, particularly when given insufficient time to exercise. Owners must be devoted to investing the necessary time and energy on a daily basis. German Shorthairs of middle age (5-6 years) and older, may be better suited to harried family lifestyles, particularly when open space is at a premium. Although German Shorthairs are highly adaptable, they are not for everyone.

Being people-oriented dogs, the German Shorthaired Pointer will bond more readily to his human family if kept indoors. If he must be kept outdoors, a small kennel run with a dog house is preferable. Dogs left alone in enclosed areas will tend to dig and may attempt to jump or climb a fence. Care should always be taken that the environment is safe when the German Shorthair is left outdoors and unattended.

When left alone for long periods of time some Shorthairs may exhibit a behavior known as separation anxiety. It tends to manifest itself in destructive behavior and excessive barking. It is

The GSP will adapt to most any living situation, however, he will bond more readily with his family if housed indoors. OTCh. Bjarke's Sargent Pepper owned by Michelle Burns.

If you introduce your German Shorthaired Pointer to other pets in your household while he is still young, he will make friends that last a lifetime.

easily overcome if owners crate-train their dogs from puppyhood so they adapt to being left alone. Failure to crate train may lead to destructive behavior in your absence.

Like all other dogs, German Shorthairs should always be supervised around young children. Shorthairs have a propensity for jumping up on people. This could be disastrous when young children or elderly relatives are involved. Dog obedience classes should be undertaken as soon as possible to try to prevent bad habits from ever occurring.

Many German Shorthaired Pointers do not get along well with cats. Behavior can vary from desire to catch and harm the cat to simple, fun chasing. If you own a cat it is best to purchase a young puppy and begin to introduce it to the cat right away.

German Shorthaired Pointers have tremendous potential to fulfill your highest expectations. They will not, however, do this without considerable effort and training on your part. A well-trained dog is a pleasure to own, whereas an untrained dog is a detriment to you and society.

STANDARD for the German Shorthaired Pointer

THE OFFICIAL STANDARD FOR THE GERMAN SHORTHAIRED POINTER

General Appearance

The German Shorthaired Pointer is a versatile hunter and an all-purpose gun dog capable of high performance in field and water. The judgement of Shorthairs in the show ring reflects these basic characteristics. The overall picture created in the observer's eye is that of an aristocratic, well-balanced, symmetrical animal with conformation indicating power, endurance and agility, and a look of intelligence and animation. The dog is neither unduly small nor conspicuously large. It gives the impression of medium size, but is like a hunter, "with a short back, but standing over plenty of ground." Symmetry and field quality are essential.

The overall appearance of a GSP should reflect power, endurance, agility, and animation.

A dog in hard and lean field condition is not to be penalized; however, overly fat or poorly muscled dogs are to be penalized. A dog well-balanced in all points is preferable to one with outstanding good qualities and defects. Grace of outline, clean-cut head, sloping shoulders, deep chest, powerful back, strong quarters, good bone composition, adequate muscle, well-carried tail and taut coat produce a look of nobility and indicate a heritage of purposefully conducted breeding.

Further evidence of this heritage is movement which is balanced, alertly coordinated and without wasted motion.

Symmetry and field quality are essential in any German Shorthaired Pointer.

Size

The height of dogs, measured at the withers, 23 to 25 inches. Height of bitches, measured at the withers, 21 to 23 inches. Deviations of one inch above or below the described heights are to be severely penalized. Weight of dogs, 55 to 70 pounds. Weight of bitches, 45 to 60 pounds.

Proportion

Measuring from the forechest to the rearmost projection of the rump and from the withers to the ground, the Shorthair is permissibly either square or slightly longer than he is tall.

Substance

Thin and fine bones are by no means desirable in a dog which must possess strength and be able to work over any type of terrain. The main importance is not so much on the size of bone, but rather on the bone being in proportion

The German Shorthaired Pointer must possess the strength and ability to work over any type of terrain.

to the body. Bone structure too heavy or too light is a fault. Tall and leggy dogs, dogs which are ponderous because of excess substance, doggy bitches, and bitchy dogs are to be faulted.

Head

The **head** is clean-cut, is neither too light nor too heavy, and is in proper proportion to the body. The **eyes** are of medium size, full of intelligence and expression, good-humored and yet radiating energy, neither protruding nor sunken. The eye is almond shaped, not circular. The preferred color is dark brown.

The German Shorthaired Pointer's head is clean cut, with dark eyes and broad flat ears.

Light yellow eyes are not desirable and are a fault. Closely set eyes are to be faulted. China or wall eyes are to be disqualified. The **ears** are broad and set fairly high, lie flat and never hang away from the head. Their placement is just above eye level. The ears when laid in front without being pulled, should extend to the corner of the mouth. In the case of heavier dogs, the ears are correspondingly longer. Ears too long or fleshy are to be faulted.

The **skull** is reasonably broad, arched on the side and slightly round on top. Unlike the Pointer, the median line between the eyes at the forehead is not too deep and the occipital bone is not very conspicious. The rise is more strongly pronounced in the dog than in the bitch. The jaw is powerful and the muscles well developed. The line to the forehead rises gradually and never has a definite stop as that of the Pointer, but rather a stop-effect when viewed from the side, due to the position of the eyebrows.

The **muzzle** is sufficiently long to enable the dog to seize game properly and be able to carry it for a long time. A pointed muzzle is not desirable. The depth is in the right proportion to the length, both in the muzzle and in the skull proper. The length of the muzzle should equal the length of the skull. A dish-shaped muzzle is a fault. A

23

definite Pointer stop is a serious fault. Too many wrinkles in the forehead is a fault.

The **nose** is brown, the larger the better, and with nostrils well opened and broad. A spotted nose is not desirable. A flesh colored nose disqualifies. The chops fall away from the somewhat projecting nose. The lips are full and deep yet are never flewy.

The **teeth** are strong and healthy. The molars intermesh properly. The bite is a true scissors bite. A perfect level bite is not desirable and must be penalized. Extreme overshot or undershot disqualifies.

Neck, Topline, Body

The **neck** is of proper length to permit the jaws reaching game to be retrieved, sloping downwards on beautifully curving lines. The nape is rather muscular, becoming gradually larger towards the shoulders. Moderate throatiness is permitted.

The **skin** is close and tight. The **chest** in general gives the impression of depth rather than breadth: for all that, it is in correct proportion to the other parts of the body. The chest reaches down to the elbows, the ribs forming the thorax show a rib spring and are not flat or slab-sided; they are not perfectly round or barrel shaped. The back ribs reach well down. The circumference of the thorax immediately behind the elbows is smaller than that of the thorax about a hand's breadth behind elbows, so that the upper arm has room for movement. Tuck-up is apparent.

The German Shorthaired Pointer's back should be short, strong, and straight. Tabor's Law N' Order, JH owned by F. Del Prete.

The **back** is short, strong, and straight with a slight rise from the root of the tail to the withers. The loin is strong, is of moderate length, and is slightly arched. An excessively long, roached or swayed back must be penalized. The hips are broad with hip sockets wide apart and fall slightly toward the tail in a graceful curve. A steep croup is a fault.

The German Shorthaired Pointer's tail should be docked, leaving it at about 40% of its natural length.

The **tail** is set high and firm, and must be docked, leaving approximately 40% of its length. The tail hangs down when the dog is quiet and is held horizontally when he is walking. The tail must never be curved over the back toward the head when the dog is moving. A tail curved or bent toward the head is to be severely penalized.

Forequarters

The **shoulders** are sloping, movable, and well-covered with muscle. The shoulder blades lie flat and are well laid back nearing a 45 degree angle. The upper arm (the bones between the shoulder and elbow joint) is as long as possible, standing away somewhat from the trunk so that the straight and closely muscled legs, when viewed from the front, appear to be parallel. Elbows which stand away from the body or are too close result in toes turning inwards or outwards and must be faulted.

Pasterns are strong, short and nearly vertical with a slight spring. Loose, short-bladed or straight shoulders must be faulted. Knuckling over is to be faulted. Dewclaws on the forelegs may be removed. The **feet** are compact, close-knit and round to spoon-shaped. The toes are sufficiently arched and heavily nailed. The pads are strong, hard and thick.

Hindquarters

Thighs are strong and well-muscled. Stifles are well-bent. Hock joints are well angulated and strong with straight bone structure from hock to pad. Angulation of both stifle and hock

The GSP's coat should be short, thick, and feel tough. It is longer on the tail and back, and shorter on the head and ears. Ch. Crossing Creeks Homesteader, owned by Ken and Judy Marden.

joint is such as to achieve the optimal balance of drive and traction. Hocks turn neither in nor out. Cow-hocked legs are a serious fault.

Coat
The hair is short and thick and feels tough to the hand; it is somewhat longer on the underside of the tail and the back edges of the haunches. The hair is softer, thinner and shorter on the ears and the head. Any dog with long hair in the body coat is to be severely penalized.

Color
The coat may be of solid liver or a combination of liver and white such as liver and white ticked, liver patched and white ticked, or liver roan. A dog with any area of black, red, orange, lemon or tan, or a dog solid white will be disqualified.

Gait

A smooth lithe gait is essential. It is to be noted that as gait increases from the walk to the faster speed, the legs converge beneath the body. The tendency to single track is desirable. The forelegs reach well ahead as if to pull in the ground without giving the appearance of a hackney gait. The hindquarters drive the back legs smoothly and with great power.

FC, AFC Timberdoodle's Holiday Edition owned by Dino and Doreen Russo demonstrates the deliberate stance of a German Shorthaired Pointer.

Temperament

The Shorthair is friendly, intelligent, and willing to please. The first impression is that of a keen enthusiasm for work without indication of nervous or flighty character.

DISQUALIFICATIONS

- China or wall eyes.
- Flesh colored nose.
- Extreme overshot or undershot.
- A dog with any area of black, red, orange, lemon, or tan, or a solid white dog.

Approved by the Board of Directors of the American Kennel Club on August 11, 1992, to be effective September 30, 1992.

INTERPRETATION OF THE STANDARD

In **general appearance** emphasis is placed on balance, as lack of balance can create undesirable illusions. General appearance defines type; one should be able to readily identify the dog as distinctly German Shorthaired Pointer, thereby differentiating it from other breeds. Muscular conditioning and clean-cut lines contribute to the overall Shorthair look.

Size, **proportion** and **substance** should be viewed as a whole; in this case, the whole is greater than the sum of the parts. While an oversized or undersized dog is undesirable, the substance should be in proportion to the size. A male Shorthair of any size, having a refined feminine head and spindly bone is undesirable, as is a female Shorthair with a masculine head and massive body and bone. It is important to relate the size standards to the rest of the body structure. Overall proportion is the ultimate goal; it is hoped that proportion can be found within the desired size.

The GSP's appearance should strike a balance between his ancestral hounds and English Pointers.

In defining the German Shorthaired Pointer **head** the standard faults heads either too closely resembling the Pointer or the hounds from which the Shorthairs originated. The clean cut lines of the Shorthair head are distinctly Shorthair. Dishy Pointer muzzles are faulted as are heavy muzzles with excess flew which would be more hound-like in appearance. In other words, the German Shorthair Pointer head should strike a balance between its ancestral hounds and English Pointers. The head should also define the sex of the dog. Males have a more pronounced rise from nose to forehead, making their heads somewhat more striking than their female counterparts.

The standard for the **neck, topline**, and **body**, carefully blends aesthetics with function. The neck should be sloping and curved, yet it is understood that the muscular nape may be throaty in appearance. The **back** is short, strong and straight, yet demands a slight rise over the loin which may be slightly arched. It is the arching that contributes to speed in the field. Back faults, particularly those that may contribute to fatigue and back disorders later in life (such as the excessively long back) are undesirable. The **tail** of the German Shorthair should be set high, but not so high that it curves back towards the head.

The clean-cut lines of the head of the German Shorthaired Pointer are distinctive in this breed. OTCh. Bjarke's Sargent Pepper owned by Michelle Burns.

The **forequarters** of the German Shorthair should be built to work a

29

long hard day in the field. Efficient movement reduces fatigue and contributes to generalized stamina. **Feet** are one of the most important working parts. A German Shorthair with loose, splayed feet will not be able to handle the heavy cover as easily as one with tightly knit feet and arched toes.

This portrait of Ch. Moraine's Diamond Lil Mariah, JH owned by Sondra Kretz portrays a wonderful example of the breed.

Balance and proportion are of greatest importance when examining the **hindquarters** of a German Shorthair. Improper balance of angles will lead to inefficient movement, and poor drive and traction.

The German Shorthaired Pointer **coat** is supposed to be water shedding and provide protection to the dog while hunting in heavy cover. The short, tight coat is best for this purpose.

The **color** standard spells out that Pointer colors are unacceptable, suggesting a recent cross breeding to a Pointer; the exception to this is the black color which has been an acceptable German Shorthaired Pointer color in Germany and most countries outside the United States. The white color is often associated with deafness, especially when it involves the head and ears. This may be the reason that an all white Shorthair is a disqualification.

Gait stresses efficiency of movement; a dog that is to work in the field needs to be able to cover ground easily. Biddability, or the willingness and desire to please are important Shorthair traits. The bubbly, outgoing, and intelligent temperament are valued characteristics of the Shorthair, and should be the goal of any breeding program.

The hindquarters of a German Shorthaired Pointer must be balanced and proportionate.

SELECTING the German Shorthaired Pointer for You

THE PROPER FIT

Now that you have decided that a German Shorthaired Pointer is the right dog for you, there are many important questions that you will have to answer before making a purchase. Choosing the right dog is somewhat like shopping for a new pair of shoes. The shoes must look good and be stylish. They must be in your price range. Most importantly, they **must fit**. You must obtain the dog that is right for you; the one that fits best. Unlike the pair of shoes which will be discarded when they become outdated, the German Shorthaired Pointer will have an average life expectancy of 12 years. As a responsible dog owner, your decision to purchase a German Shorthaired Pointer should be regarded as a commitment to care for the dog for his entire life.

The American Kennel Club has put together a "Dog Buyer's Education Packet" which includes information on acquiring a puppy, along with a geographical listing of dog clubs. The packet is informative and free and can be ordered by calling the American Kennel Club's customer service number: 919-233-9767. It may help answer some of the questions you will undoubtably have.

Will your German Shorthaired Pointer serve an additional purpose other than lifelong companion? Will he be used for hunting or field trials? Will he be shown to a championship and bred? Should you choose a male or female, or does it really matter? Would an older dog be better suited to someone in your situation?

To assist you in answering some of these questions and obtaining the "best fit," educate yourself by researching and talking to as many knowledgeable people as you can.

Be sure to do your homework and learn all you can about the breed before making the decision to bring a German Shorthaired Pointer into your home.

To ensure against genetic diseases, reputable breeders will screen all GSP's before breeding them.

PURCHASING YOUR GERMAN SHORTHAIR POINTER

The best place to purchase a German Shorthaired Pointer is from a responsible breeder. This person is committed to the breed, and has demonstrated through competition or hunting that their dogs are worthy of breeding. Most breeders will aquire the appropriate health screening on their breeding stock, prior to any breeding. They will often require a written contract with the buyer. Many breeders will take the dog back if the buyer can no longer keep it, or assist in the placement of the dog. Breeders can be located by writing to the secretary of the parent club, or through the assistance of your local veterinarian.

The American Kennel Club has a breeder referral representative program which will put you in contact with a breeder referral representative in your local community. Local kennel clubs can also be of some assistance. Some pet supply stores will also share the names of breeders with you. Attending a dog show or field trial will provide the perfect

setting in which to meet with many breeders and see their dogs.

Be prepared to be interviewed by the breeder. A good breeder wants to make sure that you are the right person for a German Shorthair. Most breeders will try to select a puppy that they believe will best meet your needs. Try not to be swayed by the colorings or markings of the pups. If a breeder refuses to sell you a dog, or politely suggests that another breed or an older dog may be more appropriate for you, take the advice seriously.

Depending upon your family's lifestyle, adopting an older dog may be the right decision for you.

Breed rescue is another avenue to pursue if you want a German Shorthaired Pointer. Rescue engages in the placement of unwanted or lost German Shorthaired Pointers that desperately need loving homes. The parent club has a national rescue chairman who can provide you with the names of local individuals involved in rescue. The advantage of dealing directly with breed rescue is that those involved will have evaluated the dogs for temperament and previous training and will make an effort to learn the dog's behavior with children, cats, and other dogs. Rescue works directly with local animal shelters. Dogs that are adopted through rescue are generally up to date on all vaccinations and neutered or spayed prior to their placement in a new home. Most rescue groups ask for a modest adoption fee to pay for the cost of the program.

"Backyard breeders" represent another source of German Shorthaired Pointers, and generally should be avoided. These are often well-intentioned individuals who happen to own a female German Shorthaired Pointer. These persons often do not know enough to determine whether their dog is a good representative of the breed. They seldom screen their dogs for inherited defects because they lack the knowledge to do so. They lack the ability

The German Shorthaired Pointer you choose should be bright-eyed, healthy, and interested in the world around him.

to assist a family who has purchased one of their puppies, and most often are unwilling or unable to take the dog back if the puppy does not work out.

35

UNDERSTANDING HEALTH SCREENING

When you go to visit a breeder, always try to observe the surroundings in which the dogs are kept. Regardless of whether they are housed indoors or out, the area should appear clean and odor-free. Observe the dam (mother) of the litter. Does she appear healthy and well cared for?

Puppies should be plump, not bony, nor pot-bellied, as this can be a possible sign of illness. A healthy puppy is well-packed. His coat should glisten. There should not be any obvious signs of infection such as discharge from the eyes or nose. Puppies should be alert and happy, responding well to people who are kneeling down at their level. Make sure that if you take one home, he is at least seven weeks of age, the minimum age for separating a puppy from his mother and litter mates.

Although no breeder can say with 100% certainty that your puppy is free of inherited defects, there are many different types of health screening available to make certain that

Your GSP will have a good start in life if his parents are happy and well adjusted. Make sure to see the dam and sire of the puppy you are considering.

dogs used for breeding are unaffected. The basic rule in dog breeding is to never start off with a sire or dam who is affected with a fault that is known to be genetic, or inherited. That would be looking for trouble. Unfortunately, many faults are recessive, which means that neither the sire nor the dam was found to be affected but both were hidden carriers. How can you protect yourself from purchasing a puppy whose parents had hidden, recessive faults? You can't. All you can ask and expect of a breeder is to have their dogs checked to ensure that their dog does not suffer from certain genetic maladies.

Ch. Moraine's Diamond Lil Mariah, JH with her newborn healthy puppy.

Hip dysplasia and inherited eye disorders, although not found with great frequency, do affect German Shorthaired Pointers. Screening is possible for both disorders. While it is useful to check all German Shorthairs for these disorders, it is imperative to check dogs that are to be used for breeding.

Hip dysplasia is a progressive developmental deformity of the hip joints. Puppies are not born with it, but in severe cases, evidence of hip dysplasia can be seen in the radiographs of four-month-old puppies. Hip dysplasia can be mild to crippling in the affected dog. It is regarded as being partly hereditary, and partly environmental, with rapid growth-rate from over-feeding being a major contributing factor.

It is a fallacy that a person can tell if a dog is dysplastic by watching him gait. Some dysplastic dogs get around remarkably well because of good muscle density and conditioning. In most cases, signs of hip dysplasia will appear in old age, if not before.

Responsible breeders will screen both sire and dam for hip dysplasia by having their hips x-rayed at the age of two, or older. The radiographs are then submitted to the Orthopedic Foundation for Animals (OFA), and dogs whose X-rays appear to be free of hip dysplasia will be given an OFA number and a rating of fair, good, or excellent. Buy puppies from breeders who can show you a copy of both the sire and dam's OFA certificate. Also ask what happens if your puppy gets hip dysplasia. Are they prepared to compensate you should that contingency arise?

Dogs are afflicted with many genetic eye disorders. Among those that may affect the German Shorthair are bilateral cataracts and entropion. In cataracts, opaque lenses develop in both eyes, usually after two years of age. This may, but does not always, lead to blindness. Surgery can be used to preserve eyesight. Entropion exists when the eyelids roll in, and rub on the cornea, creating an irritation. There is usually tearing and impaired vision from scarring; surgery is often performed to correct the condition.

Responsible breeders may opt to have their dog's eyes checked by a board certified veterinary ophthalmologist. This can usually be done during a five minute eye exam at a specially designated "eye clinic." The price to the breeder is nominal. The price of not checking dogs and breeding affected animals is catastrophic. The dog's eyes are then certified by an organization which goes by the acronym "CERF" (Canine Eye Registration Foundation). Unfortunately, just as in the case of hips, eye diseases are not always apparent to the owner, but require a skilled professional to be properly diagnosed.

German Shorthaired Pointer breeders have been a little slow to jump on the CERF bandwagon. Eye exams are mandatory protocol for many other breeds, and should be so for the Shorthair. Ask your breeder to show you a copy of the CERF certificate which includes the age of the dog, the date of his exam, his name and any identifying numbers, and that he has been found to be unaffected from any known genetic eye disorder. An eye exam should have been done within one year

A breeder should have her dogs' eyes checked and certified free of disease. Ch. Tabor's Reason to Believe has the clear dark eyes typical of a German Shorthaired Pointer.

of breeding, and must be repeated each year, as eye disorders can develop at any age.

You may have to look long and hard before you succeed in locating a breeder who screens for both hip and eye disorders, but it will be well worth the search. It is a terrible heartache to own a dog who cannot hunt, or for that

Your German Shorthaired Pointer should possess a free and easy gait in order to excel at hunting and tracking game.

Since many diseases known to the GSP are inherited, it is important that you purchase your pup from sound breeding stock that has been fully certified against congenital diseases.

matter, get around the house, because he is losing his vision. The American Kennel Club now includes the CERF and OFA certification numbers of the sire and dam on the puppy's registration application. If the breeder claims that

the dogs are certified, but it is missing from the registration application, ask to see a copy of the certificates. Puppies from breeders who screen are usually in the same price range as those who do not, so it pays to buy from those who do.

There are many other inherited disorders which may occur in the German Shorthaired Pointer, but less frequently. Some of these can also be screened in the parents. If a breeder tells you that the parents are negative for von Willebrand's disease, or subaortic stenosis (SAS), consider it useful information.

Other disorders in which heredity plays a role include: undescended testicles (crytorchidisim), deafness (associated with white color, especially white heads and ears), diabetes insipidus, panostitis, epilepsy, gastric torsion, hypothyroidism, OCD, and hermaphrodism, to name a few.

Choosing a male or female dog is a matter of preference. Either sex will make a wonderful companion.

It is hoped that this frank discussion of inherited diseases does not discourage you from purchasing a German Shorthaired Pointer. A majority of these dogs are very healthy, and with a little homework on your part, you should succeed in buying a happy and healthy dog.

MALE VS. FEMALE

The decision to choose one sex over another is largely one of personal preference. Either a male or female German Shorthaired Pointer will make a loving and loyal companion and hunting dog. Weight and size constitute the greatest difference between the two, males being 10 to 20 pounds heavier and about an inch or two taller than the females.

Breeders generally recognize that males require more time to mature than females, both physically and mentally. This could be an advantage or disadvantage, depending upon your perspective.

A female, unless spayed, will come into season approximately twice a year. During those times she must be

Breeding German Shorthaired Pointers should only be undertaken by those with the knowledge and facilities to care for all of the puppies produced.

confined to prevent an unwanted pregnancy. If she is a house dog, there is the added problem of blood-tinged stains on carpets and furniture. She also cannot hunt while in season, or compete in hunting tests and obedience trials during those periods.

Males left unneutered become easily distracted and may be challenging to train.

If you are planning to show your dog, you will have to give careful thought to your decision, as spayed and neutered dogs are ineligible for competition.

SPAYING OR NEUTERING YOUR DOG

Breeding is a responsibility that cannot be taken lightly. German Shorthaired Pointer Rescue deals with large numbers

Thousands of dogs are abandoned each year. The decision to spay or neuter your GSP will prevent any additions to the ranks of unwanted animals.

of unwanted dogs each year. Do not needlessly contribute to that number.

It would be overly optimistic to believe that you could recoup your investment or make a profit by breeding. Few people actually come out ahead after figuring in their costs. Breeding also entails the possible risk of death of the dam, some of her puppies or both. Do not breed simply to be able to keep one just like the one you own. German Shorthair litters typically are large; eight to twelve puppies is not unusual.

If breeding is a future goal, make sure you purchase a dog with proper conformation and temperament. Remember, however, there are no guarantees that this dog will turn out as anticipated. Just because a dog was sold as show stock does not mean that he is of breeding quality. Time and careful evaluation by many experienced breeders will help to confirm or disprove early expectations.

Responsible breeders may sell you a puppy with a written contract obliging you to spay or neuter your dog. Dogs that are not of breeding quality can be sold with a limited registration certificate. This means that the offspring of the dog cannot be AKC registered. Breeders try to ensure breed improvement through these methods by allowing only their top quality dogs to reproduce.

There is nothing quite as endearing as watching a mother care for her young. However, keep in mind that taking care of a litter of puppies means a lot of time and work.

Health benefits are the best reason for having your female spayed, particularly while she is young (most veterinarians recommend spaying at six months of age). Females have a lower incidence of mammary tumors (breast cancer) if spayed prior to their first heat. Unwanted pregnancies are eliminated, as are the potential infections and cancers involving the uterus and/or ovaries. Spaying will also level out hormonal fluctuations affecting temperament.

The primary reason for neutering is that it makes the male a better pet and eliminates the possibility of diseases of the male reproductive organs. This is true because intact male dogs act aggressively toward other dogs and people in an effort to protect and control their territory. The behavior is strongly influenced by male hormones. Most people find this territorial behavior unacceptable. Male dogs neutered young do not have the opportunity to become aggressive, and older dogs may also benefit from this surgery, but the outcome is less certain. Neutered dogs lose the desire to roam and will be less stressed and neurotic. Most importantly, these dogs have no chance of accidentally breeding and creating unwanted and/or unplanned puppies.

If your German Shorthaired Pointer is to work in performance activities such as hunting, hunting tests, or obedience training, she will not have to miss valuable time due to heat cycles, or in the case of the male, be distracted easily from doing his work. In most cases, spaying and neutering are the right thing to do for both you and your pet.

PUPPIES VS. OLDER DOGS

Although no one can dispute the appeal of a young pup, remember that a German Shorthaired Pointer retains his diminutive size for about three months. While most find puppies irresistibly cute and cuddly, and so much fun to own in the beginning, the fun can wear out quickly, along with the carpet, as the new puppy wears out his welcome.

There are good reasons and bad reasons to buy a puppy, as opposed to a grown dog. Among the good reasons, those who want a dog for a particular purpose, such as hunting or obedience competition, believe it is important to begin training at seven weeks of age. This is seen as the best age for human bonding to take place, even if the pup had little or no contact with people prior to that time. It is also

Puppyhood is the easiest age to socialize and train your German Shorthaired Pointer.

He may be tiny now, but a German Shorthaired Pointer will attain most of his adult size by six months of age.

recognized as the best time to begin the training process. Individuals interested in field training their dog or in placing it in show competition also like to begin working with their puppies at 7 weeks of age. Socializing a puppy for traveling and being handled by different people is a time consuming but essential step in helping the puppy to establish the self confidence required to be a trusted family companion as well as a performance dog.

Many people believe that a puppy is preferable to an older dog if there are young children in the household. Keep in mind that a German Shorthair attains most of his adult size by six months of age. By that time he will be fully capable of knocking over both children and adults. If he is to be a present for the children, remember that no matter how mature and well-intentioned your children are, the major responsibility of this dog will fall squarely on you. Young children may view a puppy as a stuffed animal, not a fragile living thing. This requires you to closely supervise your child or children around a young puppy. A young puppy will require three to four feedings a day and will need to eliminate at least every one to two hours when awake. If this pup is to become a reliable family member, time must be devoted to house training, obedience training, and general socialization. This is difficult to provide in itself, and nearly impossible to accomplish if your family consists of many young ones. It is even harder to provide if both spouses are employed outside the home. *Under no circumstances should this be viewed as the children's job*. The fascination of the puppy will be short-lived, particularly as the children are made to understand the work involved in caring for a pup.

It is probably better to wait for your children to be of school age before you consider getting a dog. A puppy is suitable, if, and only if, you are prepared to invest the time and energy needed to train and maintain him. Even though most German Shorthair pups respond well to children, it is important that the breeder assist you in selecting a pup of even temperament; one that is not made uneasy by noise and commotion, as well as the presence of young children.

If you own a cat or cats, your chances of your German Shorthaired Pointer pup accepting them are far better if you start out with a young pup. This will permit you to correct the puppy's behavior if he acts aggressively towards the cats. Full grown cats are also quite capable of correcting an overzealous pup with a swat and a hiss. There is one advantage in purchasing an older dog which is undeniable: If adult size is important to you, this is the only way you can be sure that what you see is what you get.

A slightly older German Shorthair might make just as suitable a pet for children as a pup, provided he has been properly socialized and introduced to children. Occasionally breeders will offer older dogs for sale, because they did not turn out to be the prospects

A properly socialized German Shorthaired Pointer will be a peaceful member of your household, able to get long with all the other animals in residence.

When he first arrives in your home, your new puppy will need plenty of your time and attention for training and exercise.

they had hoped for. The key to bringing in an older dog to a household with young children is knowledge of the dog's upbringing. If he has been raised properly it can save you considerable work.

If you are concerned that you are not home enough to train and properly exercise a pup, then an adult is for you. Although it is helpful to know a little bit about the dog's background, if your goal is solely to obtain a pet and you are willing to forgo knowledge about the dog's past and substitute your time and patience, then a rescue German Shorthaired Pointer may be for you. German Shorthaired Pointer Rescue can provide you with a selection of adult dogs, all deserving of loving homes. These dogs will be eternally grateful for your tender loving care, which was usually lacking in their previous home. Most will need to be trained, or re-trained, for many aspects of their new life. The ages of these dogs range from puppies to adults of 10 or 11 years. Most are two to six years of age.

REGISTRATION PAPERS

Most dogs are registered with one of the dog registries, the best known of which is the American Kennel Club. The clubs attest to the fact that the sire and dam of your puppy were purebred German Shorthaired Pointers. These registries compile records; they in no way indicate the quality of your dog. Other well known registries include the United Kennel Club, American Field, the Canadian Kennel Club, and the Kennel Club of Great Britain.

Ch. Tabor's Reason to Believe is a perfect example of good breeding.

Registration certificates are necessary if you are planning to exhibit and/or breed your dog. Most people equate registration papers with the American Kennel Club (AKC), as it is the largest and best known, and sponsors many different dog events.

When you buy a German Shorthaired Pointer that is represented as eligible for registration with the AKC, you should receive an AKC registration application properly filled out by the seller. When you submit the completed form to the AKC with the proper registration fee, you will receive an AKC registration certificate. If the dog had been registered by its previous owner or breeder you should receive the registration certificate with the reverse side completed by the owner.

If the seller cannot give you the application or registration certificate at the time of sale, and you are buying an AKC registered dog, you are entitled to a written bill of sale that includes: breed, sex, and color of dog, date of birth of dog, registered name and number of the dog's sire and dam, and the name of the breeder. If none of these is supplied, don't buy the dog.

An ILP (Indefinite Listing Privilege) number can be obtained from the American Kennel Club if

Registration papers will prove that the parents of your puppy were purebred German Shorthaired Pointers.

you adopt an unregistered German Shorthaired Pointer through breed rescue or some other source. The number will enable you to enter your dog in obedience trials, agility or tracking tests, and as of September 1, 1995, hunting tests. The AKC grants ILP numbers to unregistrable dogs of registrable breeds. Dogs eligible for an ILP number must be spayed or neutered, and must be at least six months of age. The ILP application form requests two color photographs and a copy of the spay/neuter certificate.

PEDIGREE: WHAT'S IN A NAME?

The names in your dog's pedigree may mean everything or nothing to a knowledgeable person. Just because a dog has a pedigree that can be researched and certified does not mean that the dog possesses any particular quality. Puppy mill Shorthairs may come with an AKC certified pedigree, but that in no way confers any degree of excellence. The absence of titled dogs such as champions or field champions speaks volumes about a dog's background, as does the presence of such dogs.

Much information can be gleaned from a well written and researched pedigree. A perusal of the pedigree will show you essential information about your dog. Pedigrees include the AKC registered name, number, sex of the dog, date of birth, and any titles your dog may have earned. As you move from left to right, the pedigree records the names, complete with titles earned, of the sire and dam, and then generally traces back to at least the third generation of great grandparents. Most breeders will be able to supply a pedigree of your dog that contains six generations of ancestors. If you want a pedigree that is certifiably accurate, you must order one from

When searching for a German Shorthaired Pointer puppy, do as much research as possible and avoid making a hasty decision.

the American Kennel Club. The
fee for the pedigree depends
upon the number of
generations requested.
It might be easiest to begin
with a three generation
pedigree, as the dogs listed are
likely to be of recent years, and
in many instances, alive and
functioning. You should also
look for evidence of health
screening in the pedigree such
as OFA and CERF numbers and
dates.

*Your GSP's pedigree will
offer you important
information about his
ancestry. Ch. Tabor's
Ladenfield Pebbles. Owned
by Joan and Joel Tabor.*

GUARANTEES, LEMON LAWS, AND BREEDER CONTRACTS

Lemon laws were first designed to protect consumers who
purchased defective automobiles. Puppy lemon laws presume
that purchasers should be able to recover some compensation
from commercial kennels and sellers who intentionally defraud
the public. Deceit can take the form of misrepresenting the
breed of the animal, its registration status, its age, and its
health, to name a few. Most states have existing laws to
remedy breach of contract, misrepresentation and fraud.
Lemon laws written specifically to protect buyers from
unscrupulous merchants are designed, although not always
successfully, to make enforcement less cumbersome.

Existing lemon laws guarantee against everything from
parasites to congenital defects, discovered within a few days of
purchase. Ironically, many genetic defects such as hip
dysplasia are not evident until the age of two, way beyond the
parameters of the typical lemon law. Check with your State
Department of Consumer Affairs to learn if there is a puppy
lemon law in place and exactly what it covers.

Responsible breeders are being urged to supply the buyer
with a written agreement. This contract represents a guarantee
for you, as well as protection for the breeder. An agreement
may specify the quality of the dog being sold, (ie., pet quality,
show quality, breeding quality and the sex of the dog). If the
dog being sold is pet quality, many breeders will specify that
the dog be spayed or neutered by a particular date. Failure for

the buyer to uphold that end of the agreement may render the entire guarantee null and void.

Many breeders further stipulate that the dog, if pet quality, will be sold with limited registration. This means that offspring of this dog will be ineligible for AKC registration. If the dog in question suffers from an inherited malady such as undershot or overshot jaw or cryptorchidism (one or both testicles missing from the scrotum) this should be represented on the agreement. Such defects do not make the dog less worthy as a pet, but should, under no circumstances, be used for breeding.

The agreement should specify precisely what the breeder is guaranteeing. Most breeders allow the buyer at least 72 hours to have the puppy or dog examined by their veterinarian. It is preferable that the breeder have had the dog examined by his own veterinarian prior to the sale. The breeder should have acquired a health certificate for the dog, indicating

Upon selection of your German Shorthaired Pointer puppy, the breeder should offer a guarantee against inherited disorders.

the date the dog was examined, and that it was found to be free of disease.

Some breeders will guarantee against inherited defects which develop at a later age, (i.e., hip dysplasia). This is where breeders will differ substantially. Most will accept some responsibility for the well known inherited disorders, particularly if the disorder either shortens the dog's normal life span or reduces the quality of life for the dog. As mentioned previously, undescended testicles on male puppies and improper bites will not affect the dog's longevity or substantially reduce his quality of life (except in very severe bite deformities), and therefore the only thing altered by these problems would be breeding.

Before purchasing a puppy, many breeders require you to sign a contract assuring particular aspects of his care and health maintenance.

If a dog develops an inherited defect through no fault of the breeder, most will offer to replace the dog with one of equal quality. All breeders should stipulate that the dog in question be spayed or neutered. Expensive surgeries are usually the owner's decision, unless the breeder indicates a willingness to shoulder or share some of these costs. Some breeders may place time limits on these guarantees, others will not.

Most breeders specify that the dog must be properly maintained and vetted. They may mandate fencing (usually six feet high), or invisible fencing, or some type of safe enclosure for the dog. They are only looking out for the well-being of the dog. Some contracts give breeders the right to repossess dogs that are being improperly cared for. Most breeders want you to agree that if you can no longer keep the dog it must be returned to them, or they must approve a transfer of ownership. If all breeders did this there would not be an overpopulation of unwanted German Shorthaired Pointers in animal shelters, and German Shorthaired Pointer Rescue would be unnecessary.

Written contracts should also state the date inoculations were given. Dates of the last worming should be noted as well as what parasites the dog had been previously treated for. Diet should be mentioned—how much and what type of food.

The American Kennel Club warns people to give thought before entering into a co-ownership. These entanglements generate the most frequent complaints to the AKC. There is nothing wrong with a co-ownership per say, but before agreeing to one the buyer must have a full understanding of the agreement and feel willing and able to work with the breeder. Be sure to have the entire co-ownership agreement written out; the buyer and breeder should each retain a copy for their records.

Temperament testing will tell a lot about a pup's personality. A GSP puppy should seem interested and inquisitive about his surroundings.

Dogs that are sold as show dogs are commonly put out on co-ownerships, which are sometimes referred to as breeder's terms. Do not agree to breed your dog and give the breeder their pick of the litter unless you are thoroughly committed to showing or competing with your dog in obedience or the field. Be sure that breeding is something you can handle when the time comes around. Breeders should specify that dogs that are to be used for breeding must first have their hips and eyes checked. If the dog does not screen out, it should be spayed or neutered.

Before any contract is signed you must feel comfortable and trust your breeder. No matter how well a contract is written, it may be difficult to enforce. The responsible breeder should use a written agreement to demonstrate good faith.

Temperament Testing

At seven weeks of age a puppy is ready to be removed from the litter and adapt to his new "human pack." A puppy who has dominated his littermates will attempt to establish himself as leader of his new human family. He may growl or nip anyone who corrects his behavior, grooms, bathes, or clips his toenails. He will be particularly defensive when anyone tries to remove his food, bones or play toys. These behaviors indicate that the puppy has not been properly assigned his subordinate role in the "human pack."

Your GSP puppy will look to you, his owner, to take care of his needs.

Many breeders try to objectively evaluate each puppy before he leaves to join his new family. This prevents problems like a dominant dog going to a family that has no prior experience with dogs. To this end, the breeder employs one of many temperament tests.

If temperament tests are to be meaningful, the testing of all the puppies should be completed on the same day. A stranger is invited to implement the test and it should be performed in a new location for the puppies. Some tests require values to be assigned to each of the puppy's responses using a scoring system of one to ten. Scores in the nine to ten range may demonstrate dominance, etc. Moderate scores would be preferred for the inexperienced dog owner.

Temperament tests should evaluate the following: the puppy's willingness to accept human dominance (measured by how long and hard a puppy will struggle when restrained or put in a subordinate position); his response to pain (high threshold to pain may be a hard dog to train); his desire to please (measured by his willingness to come when called); his independence (whether he follows the tester or goes off exploring); his sensitivity to noise; his pointing instinct; and his retrieval instinct. Do not rely solely on these tests because they are not perfect; they are crude estimates of a puppy's temperament and work best when combined with the daily observations of the breeder. A puppy may be experiencing an "off" day when the test is conducted, skewing the scores. The breeder should be aware if a puppy's regular behavior does not conform to the tested pattern.

Older dogs should go through a similar temperament evaluation. Noted dog trainer, behaviorist, and author Carol Lea Benjamin modified a puppy evaluation test to accommodate dogs of all ages.

Playfulness and activity are often signs of a well-socialized and well-adjusted puppy.

The twelve observations of her test include: reacting to a new environment, getting the dog's attention, following, coming when called, willingness to accept affection, teaching the dog to sit, aggressiveness with other dogs, reaction to children, observing the level of dominance, observing the activity level, retrieving instinct, and relating to cats.

When choosing your German Shorthaired Pointer, watch him carefully. The way he behaves will tell you a lot about his temperament.

They say curiosity killed the cat, but in the case of a GSP puppy, it's a good thing. A puppy who is aware and curious will be an intelligent companion and a quick learner.

Temperament evaluation assists in fitting the puppy or dog to his new owner or family. Dogs purchased with the intent of hunting or field trialing should be inquisitive, bold, score medium to high in dominance, medium to high pain threshold (a very sensitive

dog may crumble under training pressure), demonstrate desire to please yet display some degree of independence, exhibit low sensitivity to noise, and a great desire to point and retrieve. German Shorthaired Pointers that score high in dominance are termed "alpha" dogs and should never be placed with young children or inexperienced people. A dominant dog is not necessarily an evil dog. These dogs have difficulty accepting control and require a firm hand and plenty of training. Owners must be carefully matched. Hyperactive dogs belong in homes with large amounts of property and equally active owners (jogging is a great energy equalizer), and preferably should be worked in the field, obedience, and agility training.

Like mother, like daughter. Oftentimes, the temperament of a puppy will be much like her parents.

On the other hand, shy dogs should go to quiet homes with no children and few demands. Each dog has a compatible match.

Socialization

Researchers have learned that puppies devoid of all human contact between the ages of three to sixteen weeks of age developed a fear of people. If placed in a situation with people they would run or huddle in a corner trembling and might attempt to snap or bite if approached.

This extreme example demonstrates the need for puppies to be regularly handled by people at an early age if they are to become companion animals. Experienced breeders recognize the importance of early handling by providing physical, then later social, stimulation for the pups.

When you purchase a puppy at seven weeks of age, it is up to you to continue to provide enriching experiences to help the puppy overcome any shy tendencies and expand his horizons. Owners with busy lifestyles with long hours and busy schedules may

A German Shorthaired Pointer destined for life in the field must be especially stalwart, inquisitive, and bold.

unintentionally neglect their pup. Dogs who are left by themselves and seldom see others or travel away from their property suffer from poor stimulation and socialization.

An owner can do several things to stimulate and enrich his puppy. First, try not to leave your puppy isolated for prolonged periods of time. In nature pups would never be left alone. When left alone outdoors for extended periods a pup will dig, chew, scratch and sometimes bark. Indoors, the puppy may destroy furniture or have house training accidents. Introduce him to people of all ages, both men and women. Expose him to many new situations but be sure that these are enriching experiences. Experiences should provide the puppy with opportunities to investigate and interact with others. Take your pup on trips to parks, shopping centers, and obedience and agility classes for stimulating experiences.

Chasing a ball may provide useful exercise but it is not a substitute for outings which provide opportunities for interaction and investigation. If your puppy acts hesitant or fearful during these outings, use a treat to distract him. "Over-mothering" a puppy who demonstrates shyness is equally as bad as excessive discipline. Praise and treat your puppy for going forward and prevent him from hiding out.

It is important not to leave your puppy unoccupied for long periods of time. A puppy needs stimulation and activity to develop into a well-socialized adult.

Encourage your puppy to question and explore the world around him. New experiences will enrich his life and make him an active participant in his own socialization.

Within his new home, encourage him to explore steps, vacuum cleaners, cars, baths and grooming. Food rewards can be used here as well for distraction. Begin collar training your pup with a soft buckle collar. When he is comfortable with the collar, begin leash training. After he has become accustomed to walking around with the leash dragging, pick up the leash and let the pup lead you. Coax the puppy to follow you by bending down and using food rewards. All these things should be done gradually so as not to overwhelm your pup. As your puppy begins to explore new things and learns that they won't hurt him, he will be more eager the next time around.

If you purchase an older dog, try to determine if he has been properly socialized. If he is over 16 weeks and still unsocialized it is highly unlikely he will overcome his fears. On the other hand, adopting a well-socialized adult dog can save you the time and energy that you would have had to invest in the enrichment process.

CARING for Your German Shorthaired Pointer

YOU ARE WHAT YOU EAT: DETERMINING PROPER DIET

German Shorthaired Pointers excel on a high-quality dry food diet. Nutritionally, dry foods are equal in quality to canned foods but are far less expensive. Their abrasive effect helps to decrease dental tartar in many dogs. There are three types of dry dog food: kibble, meal and expanded. A kibbled food is slow baked in a sheet, then broken into small pieces called kibbles. Meal mixes prepare dry ingredients together. Expanded dog foods are cooked in an extruder and then forced through a dye, which results in expansion. The majority of dog foods are of the expanded type.

Professional type dog foods that are sold in pet or feed stores generally offer a full product line of food geared to your dog's age and activity level. The quality of the food is independent of the form. The analysis of ingredients are broken down by percent of contents, and all ingredients must be listed in descending order of predominance. This permits you to make comparisons between different brands and different formulas within brands. Expect to pay more for high protein and high fat foods, as these ingredients cost the manufacturer more.

Many dog foods advertise that they meet the NRC (National Research Council) requirements. These requirements

German Shorthaired Pointers require some vegetable matter in their diet. The CARROT BONE™, made by Nylabone®, helps

control plaque, eases the need to chew, and is nutritious. It is highly recommended as a healthy toy for your German Shorthaired Pointer.

represent the **minimum** amount of nutrients needed. Advertising that a dog food meets NRC requirements can be misleading. A diet adequate for older or inactive dogs would be deficient for the high energy requirements of younger dogs. Most breeders can provide a list of high-quality dog foods they recommend. All selections should be based on your dog's age and special energy needs, which may change seasonally.

Consult your breeder or veterinarian about the appropriate diet for your German Shorthaired Pointer.

There are a number of quality dog foods available that will offer special nutritional value to your growing puppy.

Puppies should be kept on puppy food at least through 16 weeks of age. Most people feed puppy food until the dog has reached full height, which occurs between six months to a year and a half. It is

imperative if you use a high quality, highly digestible food containing all the nutrients to permit maximum growth rate, that you do not overfeed. The rapidly growing German Shorthaired Pointer will be more predisposed to skeletal problems if you overfeed. Always keep an eye on the dog's "waistline." There should be an indentation through his loin. Dogs that are too fat usually develop a fat pad immediately in front of the base of the tail. If your dog has skin folds, he has been fed too generously. Keep your dog lean.

Baths are only required occasionally for a GSP, but be sure to use a shampoo specially formulated for dogs.

Try to stick with one brand of food. Although treats such as dog biscuits can be used for training and as snacks, they should not constitute a major portion of the diet. Switching dog foods frequently, or pandering to your dog by adding "people food" to their diet will only make him picky and may lead to digestive problems.

Establish regular feedings, usually three times a day until your dog is 16 weeks of age. Afterwards, two meals a day will be sufficient. Your dog will look forward to these feedings. It has been found that smaller, divided meals are actually better for your dog than one big meal. Gastric torsion, or bloat, occurrs more frequently when dogs are fed only one large meal.

GROOMING YOUR GERMAN SHORTHAIRED POINTER

German Shorthairs are often referred to as "spit and polish" dogs; their grooming requirements are minimal, particularly when compared with other breeds. Like all dogs, they do require regular care.

A healthy German Shorthaired Pointer should have a rich, shiny coat. A dry, brittle coat with flaky skin may be an indication that your dog requires attention. Your dog will benefit from a

If you accustom your puppy to grooming procedures at an early age, he will come to think of it as a pleasant experience.

once a week going over with a rubber curry. In addition to the rubber curry there are a variety of grooming mitts available; those made of rubber with rubber teeth (similar to the rubber curry), or those of sisal, work well. A shedding blade is useful during seasonal coat changes to assist in dead hair removal. Pumice stone can also be used for this purpose.

Baths will also assist in extracting loose, dead hair as well as dirt. Use a shampoo that is formulated for dogs, as their PH balance differs from humans. Medicated shampoos are iodine based or tar based. Either is good if your dog is suffering from dry skin, provided he is not allergic to the compounds. Flea shampoos made from pyrethrin have low toxicities and do a good job in flea control. There are also citrus-based shampoos which are natural insect repellents. Most of these repel but do not kill fleas, so your selection should depend upon the level of infestation. Ticks usually require a stronger shampoo or dip. Read all labels carefully before applying, as some of these preparations are quite toxic.

Creme rinses can be used after shampooing and are useful in preventing dry skin and dandruff. Dogs should not be bathed more than once a week, as over-bathing will cause dry coat and skin. Chronic dry coat and skin may indicate that your dog requires a diet higher in fat. Coat supplements designed for dogs and given internally may help. If you have tried these remedies and your dog continues to have a coat and/or skin problem, he should be seen by a veterinarian.

German Shorthaired Pointers have the type of ear flaps that parasites, fungi, and bacteria like best—long flaps with little exposure to air. The dark moist condition can lead to ear

During grooming, examine your German Shorthaired Pointer carefully for any signs of parasites he may have contracted outdoors.

infections or ear mites. Ears may be cleaned regularly with cleansing preparations, or mineral oil. Ask your veterinarian to demonstrate the method for cleaning the ears. To avoid infection, pay special attention to drying inside the ear canal after bathing or swimming. Signs of ear infection include head shaking of a constant nature, pawing at the ears, or dirty malodorous matter in the ears.

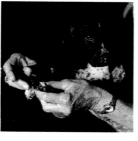

Establish a grooming routine early in your dog's life. Procedures like nail clipping will be far easier with a willing participant.

German Shorthaired Pointer's ears are prone to infection. Be sure to thoroughly clean his ears as part of your grooming routine.

Toenails should be trimmed at least once every month. Learn how to do it yourself. A toenail clipper of either the guillotine style or spring loaded type works well. Keep a

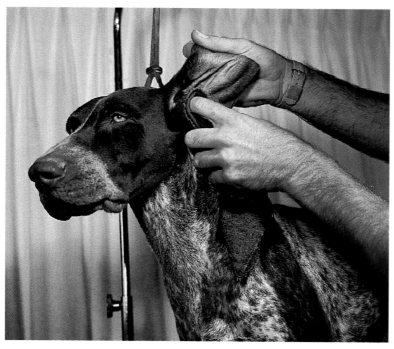

container of nail clotting powder on hand just in case you hit the quick of the nail. Some prefer the electric grinder (hobby type tool); use either the sand paper disc or stone attachments. It will be easiest if someone can assist you by holding the dog. Clipping the quick of the nail can be quite painful to the dog, so try to avoid cutting too close to this sensitive area.

The German Shorthaired Pointer is an extremely energetic dog. They will require plenty of exercise and activity outdoors.

EXERCISING YOUR GERMAN SHORTHAIRED POINTER

German Shorthaired Pointers are an extremely active breed. Although adaptable to many different living situations, they must be given ample opportunity to expend energy.

Their activity needs will vary with their age and individual temperament. Even a low-key puppy, if confined for many hours during the day, will require several hours of vigorous exercise, in divided intervals. Puppies and young Shorthairs should have a safe area, preferably one that is fenced, where they can run off-lead. If this is not possible, there are several different types of long lines available which can serve this purpose.

The 16 foot and 26 foot extending leashes have become popular in recent years. These leashes automatically expand or recoil with the movement of your dog. The non-expanding long lines are of canvas or nylon, and available in 10', 15', 20', and 30' lengths. They are a little more cumbersome to handle but are preferred by many obedience trainers and can also be used for basic field training.

Exercising a young GSP should be an interactive experience. They will enjoy roughhousing, playing fetch, brisk walking (particularly in the woods or fields), and jogging, although be careful not to over exert a young puppy. Vigorous exercise should include a warm-up and a cool-down time. Formal obedience training should begin as soon as your puppy has had all his vaccinations, which is usually at four months. Off-leash running requires a relatively obedient dog. The sooner your dog has mastered basic obedience, the sooner you will be able to let him run in safe areas, off-lead.

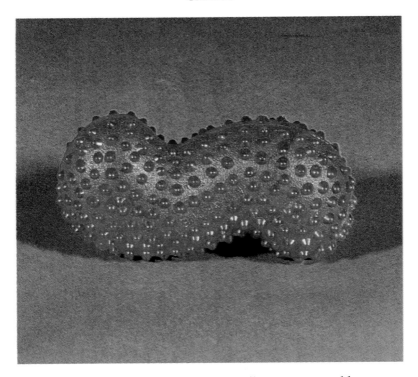

The HERCULES™ is made of very tough polyurethane. It is designed for German Shorthaired Pointers who are extremely strong chewers. The raised dental tips massage the gums and mechanically remove the plaque they encounter during chewing.

Not all exercise need be vigorous. All German Shorthairs and their owners can benefit from on-leash walks. In addition to allowing your dog to relieve himself, walks may be used to help socialize him to sights, sounds, people, and other dogs in your neighborhood.

If you have a dog pen, or enclosed area that your dog uses to relieve himself, remember that it does not substitute for off-leash running or on-leash walking. It is merely convenient for you. Try not to neglect your dog by leaving him confined for long periods of time. Undesirable behavior is likely to result from lack of attention. Never leave your dog in an enclosure wearing a choke collar because, unfortunately, dogs have been known to accidentally strangle themselves.

ACCOMMODATIONS

Your dog will require a safe place to stay when you are out of the house. A dog crate or cage will provide the proper accommodations. The dog crate is a den-like enclosure and will immediately reduce separation anxiety. Puppies become very accepting of a dog crate when introduced to it at a young age.

The first introduction to the crate can be accomplished by propping the door open and leaving favorite dog toys or treats inside. Some feed their dog inside their crate so that the associations made with it will be pleasant. Metal or fiberglass dog crates are moderately priced and well-suited for confining your dog in your absence. They are also useful when traveling and constitute the safest way to transport your dog (similar to a child safety seat). What is particularly nice about a crate is that it is mobile. Some fold up like a suitcase and can be taken along with you on vacation or visiting friends.

Crates can be a dog's best friend. Aside from providing your GSP with a safe haven, they are also useful when traveling.

Many people feel that it is cruel to confine a dog to a crate. It *is* cruel if the dog has not been properly introduced to the crate and trained, but if done properly, your pup will prefer it for sleeping or when left alone. Dogs exhibited in the show ring or run at field trials must accept being crated, particularly when being transported.

If your German Shorthair is to spend some or all of the day outdoors unattended, he must be placed in a safe enclosure. The recommended height for fencing is six feet. Some German Shorthairs possess climbing and/or jumping skills, necessitating a top on the kennel. A five by ten by six-foot-high enclosure will provide the bare minimum requirements for holding a dog. It should not be thought of as a place to exercise your dog. Larger runs can allow for exercising as well.

The run should contain a dog house to provide protection from the elements. The dog house should be elevated off the ground and insulated if he will be spending any time outdoors in inclement weather. Dog houses may be constructed out of wood that has been waterproofed or prefabricated fiberglass. The fiberglass houses are nearly indestructible and are thoroughly washable. They are also more insect-proof than wood. The house should be large enough to permit your dog to stand up in and turn around, but not so large as to decrease energy

Although "Max" is small now, it is important to remember that any outdoor enclosure you choose for him must accommodate him when he is full grown.

efficiency, and it should keep your dog sufficiently warm in cold weather. Remember that your German Shorthaired Pointer will bond more readily to his human family if housed indoors.

Kennel runs and enclosures are best used to contain your dog during the day when you are away from home. Full yard fencing will provide a safe area to play, train, and exercise your dog, and some may use it as a convenient area for the dog to relieve himself. Fencing should be six feet high. Invisible fencing, which relies on radio waves, may also be used to contain your dog on your property. Invisible fencing may provide the answer to landscaping problems where a fence may be unsightly. It should be remembered, however, that although it may keep your dog within your boundaries, it will not keep other dogs, cats, or wildlife out of your yard. Dogs should not be left outside unsupervised in any yard.

As your dog grows older he will appreciate a draft-free, well-padded place to sleep. Pet supply shops sell many different types of dog beds that meet the necessary requirements. Puppies and young dogs may also be trained to sleep in a dog bed after they have been thoroughly crate-trained and housebroken. Do not place the dog bed in the crate, as it may be destroyed. A crate pad, old blanket, or towel that can be discarded if ripped may be better suited for the crate.

Make sure your dog is kept in a secure fenced-in area when he is unsupervised.

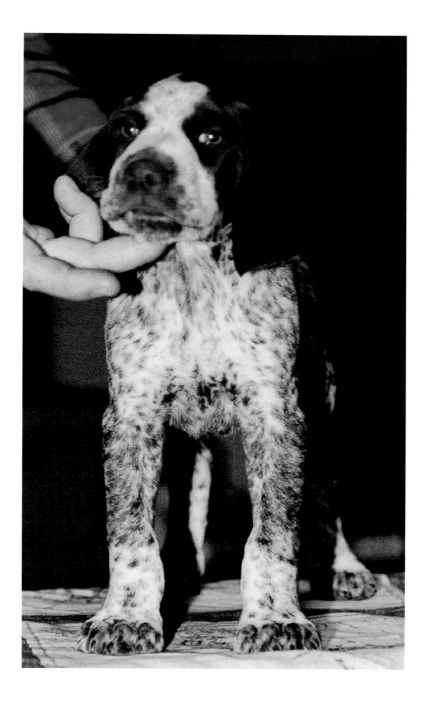

HOUSEBREAKING and Training Your GSP

HOUSEBREAKING/CRATE TRAINING

The crate is the best method available to housebreak a dog of any age, although most trainers would agree that it is more acceptable to the dog when introduced to him as a puppy. It is important to remember that a puppy must be taught to be comfortable in his crate.

When setting up your pet's crate, it is important to place it away from family members. If your dog is not housetrained you may wish to place the crate in your bedroom at night so that he has social contact and can alert you should he need to be taken out. During the day, the crate should be placed in or near areas such as the kitchen or family room. It should be located in a corner or niche that is free of drafts and direct heat.

Buy a crate that will be large enough to accommodate your dog when he is full grown. This means that he should be able to lie down on his side, sit, stand and turn around with reasonable comfort when he is mature. Usually the sizes that conform to a full grown German Shorthaired Pointer are wire crates with the approximate measurements of 36"L x 22-24"W x 26" H. If you are purchasing the crate for a puppy you will need a piece of plywood, masonite, or wire as a partition. Some wire crate manufacturers now have partitions available to fit their crates.

Introduce the crate to your dog by feeding him in it with the door open. Between feedings, place dog treats inside the crate and praise him if he enters the crate to eat the food. After the puppy or dog willingly enters the crate (which may take several days), close the crate door while he is eating. After he has completed eating, or after 20 minutes, remove the food dish. Don't leave food or water in the crate. Remove the puppy from the crate and immediately take him outside to relieve himself. If he is small, carry him outside to avoid an accident on the way. If the walk is successful, praise the puppy or dog for eliminating and let him stay outside with you or in a confined area of the house with you for a short play period—

about 15 minutes for puppies and one hour for adult dogs. If the walk was nonproductive, return him to the crate. After play time, crate the puppy or dog until the next walk.

Always offer the dog a small treat for entering the crate; this leads to a positive association for the dog. Create a workable schedule of every two to three hours for young puppies, and every four to five hours for adults. You will increase the intervals when your puppy or dog demonstrates control. The schedule is feed, water, walk, play.

You may place bedding inside the crate, using such materials as an old blanket, towel, or artificial lambskin rug. If your dog destroys these, remove them and leave the crate bare. Do not put newspapers in the bottom of the crate. Leave at least two chewing toys in the crate to occupy him. Some people find that leaving a radio on provides solace to the dog. When you first begin to crate train it is important that your dog learns that being quiet in the crate leads to safety. He must not be permitted to bark, whine or howl. Leave the

The GALILEO™ is the toughest nylon bone ever made. It is flavored to appeal to your German Shorthaired Pointer and has a relatively soft outer layer. It is a necessary chew toy and doggy pacifier.

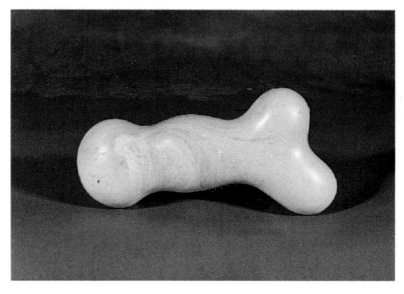

room but stay nearby to monitor his behavior. If he begins to bark, cry, or whine, intervene with a sharp, "No." Sometimes you may have to strike the top of his crate with a rolled up newspaper. It may take several visits before he stops fussing.

After about 30 to 45 minutes has transpired without any fussing, a subsequent outburst may indicate a need to go outside to relieve himself. Take him outside, praise him when he has eliminated, and allow him some play time outside the crate.

Puppies will have to eliminate upon waking, shortly after eating, and after playing. Young puppies may not be able to sleep through the whole night without having to urinate, so be prepared to be awakened during the night.

In order to facilitate house training, try to feed and water a young dog no later than six o'clock. You may withhold water the remainder of the evening.

Clean the crate and the dog anytime there is an accident. Be sure you are taking him out frequently enough. Did you fail to respond to your dog's cue? You may be feeding and watering your dog too much or too often. House training accidents are your fault, not the dog's. Never rub a dog's nose in his own excrement as it will accomplish nothing and only serve to confuse the dog.

What happens if during play time your dog has an accident? If you catch him in the act, tell him, "No," then take him outside to complete the act. Praise him when he has eliminated. If the dog had an accident which you discover several hours after the fact, there is nothing you should do but clean up the mess. Puppies have short-term memories. They have already forgotten what they did so there is no sense in punishing them.

Although it may sound complicated, crate training is the simplest and fastest method to accomplish housetraining. Stay with it and you will see how quickly it is possible to increase the intervals between exercising. As your dog becomes trained, allow him more free time outside the crate where you can carefully monitor him. Be sure to leave the crate door open should he get tired and go in there on his own for a nap.

Expect some mistakes in the beginning. Be sure to clean the area with a product designed to clean and neutralize the odor. (These products are sold in pet supply stores.) If your dog continues to go back to the same area, you have not removed the scent and need to clean it more thoroughly. If your dog begins to have frequent mistakes you probably have progressed too fast and may have to backtrack.

Be sure that you are not overusing the crate. Your dog should not be crated for long periods of time on a regular basis, particularly without having the opportunity to get out and exercise in between. It is vitally important that your dog receive human interaction and love. The crate is only a tool for making your dog a better companion.

EARLY BASIC TRAINING

A dog does not understand what we call right and wrong; this is something he must be taught. Untrained dogs will get into garbage, chew on furniture, jump up on people, etc. If you do not want the dog to engage in undesirable activities, you must correct the objectionable behavior while it is happening, not after the fact. This means that until your dog has been trained and is past his adolescence, (when he is likeliest to get into trouble), he must be under your watchful eye. If you can't watch him, crate him. Don't take the chance that the dog will get into trouble that you were unable to correct.

Puppies are naturally mischievous and playful. Early basic training will be much more successful if you make it fun and interesting.

Avoid hitting the puppy. It will cause him to be hand shy. Decide what will and will not be permitted, then consistently enforce those rules. Don't encourage your puppy to nibble at your hands one minute while scolding him the next. Correct the undesired behavior with "No." As soon as he has stopped the undesirable behavior, praise him lavishly.

You can create some of your own training tools. A throw can requires an empty aluminum soda can with a dozen or so pennies or nuts and bolts in it and a piece of tape across the opening. It produces a sound if shaken or thrown which most dogs find unpleasant. An empty squirt bottle can be filled with water and sprayed at the dog if caught in the act of an undesirable behavior. A beanbag can be made using dried beans and an old sock. This can be hurled at your dog in order to frighten, but not hurt, him. Make sure that all discipline is immediately followed by praise and reassurance.

German Shorthaired Pointers are notorious for investigating everything with their mouths. In order to prevent chewing problems you must channel your dog's energy into chewing

Electronic collars can be used to aid in training or control barking. However, they are only useful if implemented carefully.

something acceptable. Pups have a great need to chew during teething at three to four months, and when the permanent teeth become set in the jaw, between six and twelve months. Puppies and dogs should be given an ample supply of dog items designed for chewing such as Nylabone®, sterilized bones, and Roarhide® bones. When a pup begins chewing on something he shouldn't, just remove the object. Follow this by immediately offering one of his chews, and praise him.

Dogs bark for a variety of reasons. Sometimes the dog is trying to tell you that there is something unusual on the property. Territorial barking is normal, and even desirable, to some extent. Continued uninterrupted barking is undesirable and should be discouraged. Correct the dog verbally, but if the barking continues, use the throw can, beanbag, or spray bottle to enforce your command.

If you leave your German Shorthaired Pointer outside all day he may become a problem barker. Some people resort to the electronic no-bark collar. These collars emit a low level electrical impulse upon sensing vibrations from the dog's vocal cords. Most dogs will yelp when they receive the impulse and may bark several more times until they realize that only when they bark do they receive a shock. No-bark collars are expensive and will not cure the cause of the problem, such as separation anxiety. The collars are useful, however, when barking becomes intolerant.

The most dangerous type of barking occurs when directed towards his owner, especially when being disciplined.

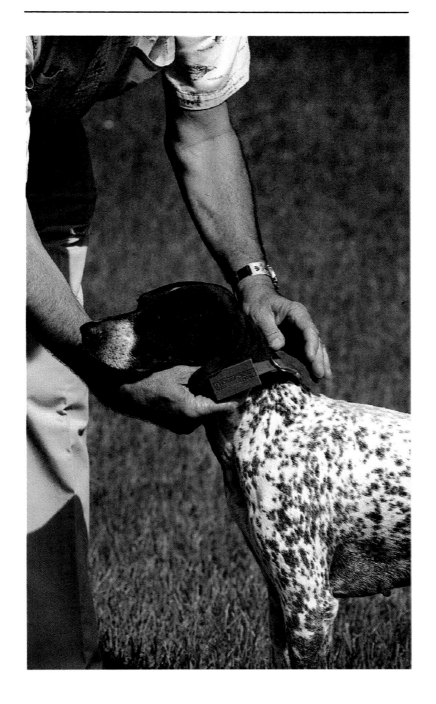

Oftentimes, a young puppy's barks or growls are overlooked because they seem cute or harmless. In fact they are neither. Uncontrolled barking, particularly when directed towards people, may precede a biting problem, and is undesirable behavior.

OBEDIENCE TRAINING FOR YOUR GERMAN SHORTHAIRED POINTER

All dogs and owners profit from basic obedience training. It is generally recommended that training begin between four to six months of age, or when the pup is housetrained and has completed his vaccinations. You should begin very basic training as soon as you get your puppy. Teach your puppy to sit, come when called, and to walk nicely on a leash without tripping you or pulling you. You will be setting important groundwork for his formal training.

A basic obedience rule is to give a command once and expect the puppy to respond. People who repeat a command three times are training their dog to respond on the third command. Basic obedience training consists of sit, come when called, stand, down, stay and heel or controlled walking.

Early training for pups is referred to as puppy kindergarten and involves more socialization than actual training. German Shorthaired Pointers may present a challenge in training, as they tend to be both stubborn and sensitive. They may respond poorly to training methods which depend heavily upon correcting behavior in a forceful manner. Learn to implement positive training methods that rely heavily on food rewards. The German Shorthair is usually very food-motivated, making this method more pleasurable for owner and dog alike.

Training can take place with a group or in private, either at home or at the training facility. Private lessons are more expensive, but do

Group training sessions will allow your puppy to make friends and are a wonderful way to continue your puppy's socialization.

Very basic training can begin at a relatively early age, once a puppy has been vaccinated and housebroken.

have the obvious advantage of being one-on-one. Group lessons, however, have their advantages as well. In a group setting, a dog must learn to behave around other dogs and other people. These distractions prove valuable in training. You would do better to begin training in a group and use private lessons only if you need help with a specific problem.

It is not unusual to hear owners comment that their dogs listen perfectly at home, but tend to disobey in class. Check out local training clubs, adult education classes, and private training schools. The private training schools often offer superior training, but each class needs to be individually evaluated. Inquire about the number of dogs and trainers in one class. You may ask about the training methods that are employed, and ask if you may come and observe a class. Inquire about the qualifications of the trainer(s). These are reasonable requests, and the quality of your pet's training depends upon thorough investigation.

Proper equipment for training includes a six-foot leash, preferably of leather. A snug fitting chain choker with medium weight links is generally recommended, but your trainer may recommend a prong-type training collar after evaluating your dog. Do not use this collar on your dog unless an experienced trainer is assisting you. This is not as cruel a tool as it may look, and in many cases it is more humane and effective than a chain choke.

Ch. Up 'N Adam's Captain Marvel, CDX, JH and Ch. Cheza-Sherwood's Morning Mist owned by Michelle Burns, at work in the field.

A dog well-trained in basic obedience commands will take about another year of regular training before he has reached a level of competency. Do not expect to have a perfectly well-mannered dog after an eight week obedience session. German Shorthairs may be more easily distracted than other dogs in your class. Remember that each dog is an individual and will learn at his own rate. Dogs understand obedience commands in far less time, but it takes a year to attain reliability. If you plan to start formal training at the age of six months and train consistently, you may have a well-trained dog at one and one half years of age.

INTRODUCTION TO FIELD TRAINING

Before a puppy can learn to hunt, he must learn to respond to basic commands, the most basic of which is to come when called. Basic socialization skills, discussed elsewhere, are also essential to creating a confident dog. While German Shorthairs were bred for their versatile hunting ability, they should not be used for hunting without proper training.

If you are starting with a young puppy under 12 weeks of age, you might try to introduce a bird wing on a fishing pole to arouse his pointing instincts. Don't overdo the bird wing as this is sight pointing. Eventually, you will be training your dog to scent point. A knotted towel, or small canvas bumper can be used to encourage retrieving. A child's cap gun may be fired when the object is tossed. In lieu of a cap gun, clap loudly with your hands. Always praise

Nylabone® toys are perfect for use when introducing retrieving to your puppy.

the puppy when he retrieves the object. Do not overdo any training as a puppy has an attention span of five to ten minutes at most. It is better to repeat these sessions several times a day.

When the puppy is three months old, he should be taken on field outings on a weekly basis, where he can be encouraged to find, flash point and chase birds. His basic obedience training and yard work should continue. In addition to "Come," the puppy should be taught "No," "Fetch," and "Whoa." It is useful to train the dog to both hand and whistle signals as well as verbal commands. This is also an excellent age to introduce a young dog to water if there is a pond or lake accessible to you. A water retrieving dummy can be thrown in the water on a long line to encourage the pup to go in and fetch. Most German Shorthairs are great water dogs when introduced to water early in life.

Live birds can be used to train a puppy at six months of age. Many trainers begin with live pigeons which are both less expensive and hardier than hand raised game birds. A dead pigeon can be used to practice retrieving. German Shorthairs will generally tire of pigeons at some point and will need to work on planted game birds as well as pigeons.

All dog training involves repetition, association, and positive reinforcement. A 30 foot-check cord may be used to enforce some commands. It is useful even if the dog is dragging it on the ground as it provides the owner a handle to grab, should that be necessary. Shock collars are sometimes useful in field training in select situations. Unfortunately, many people think that the collar will train the dog and look to it to hasten the training process. If the dog does not understand the command, the collar will rarely help. When the dog knows what is

Training a dog for the field can be difficult and time consuming, but the effort is well worth it. Misty, Captain, and Angel show off the fruits of their labor.

expected of him, the collar may be used when all other forms of correction are out of range.

One of the advantages of the collar is that the dog does not associate you with the correction. Many fine Shorthairs have been ruined by a well-meaning owner who thought he had discovered the quick road to success by either overusing the collar, using it in inappropriate situations, or turning the intensity up too high. Shock collars *do* have their place in the arsenal of training equipment, but only as a tool.

You can begin training your German Shorthaired Pointer with live game at about six months of age. Three-year-old Ch. Tabor's Ajax JH owned by George and Karen Heaney proudly presents his catch.

Training a young dog for the field is difficult and time consuming. Try to keep a slow pace. It is easier to speed up than it is to backtrack once damage has been done. If a dog develops a negative association with one phase of his training, it takes considerable effort to undo the damage. Don't forget to praise your dog when he does what he is supposed to, particularly after you have corrected him.

Gun shyness is a manmade problem. Some dogs exhibit greater noise sensitivity than others. Begin early on with the cap gun and keep the associations positive. When the dog is not bothered by that noise, you may proceed to a low caliber blank gun. If at any time during its use the dog displays uneasiness, backtrack. Also make sure that the dog is intently involved in something else and is not focusing on the noise. When a low caliber blank can be fired without any apparent nervousness, you can increase the caliber of the blanks. Eventually your dog will be ready to handle the sound of a shot gun blast.

Once your dog has learned such basics as "Whoa" and is steady to the flush, it is time to take him hunting during open season. Your dog will still have a long way to go before being a polished bird dog. It will be up to you to decide how far along you are going to train your dog. Many people need to rely upon the help of a professional at this point—if not sooner. If you decide that you are going to train the dog entirely by yourself, read as many good books on field training as possible. There are also many excellent videos available that can assist you.

SPECIAL ROLES FOR GERMAN SHORTHAIRED POINTERS

The combined intelligence, athleticism, scenting ability, and strong desire to please, make the German Shorthaired Pointer suitable for many different purposes.

Some German Shorthaired Pointers have been trained to do search and rescue work. This involves locating lost persons, or persons who may be buried in debris as a result of a disastrous event. The German Shorthair's superior tracking ability enables him to perform this type of work.

The less energetic German Shorthairs may be well-suited for therapy dog work. This involves visiting nursing homes, senior centers, rehabilitation centers, and hospitals, for the purpose of interacting with the patients. Dogs used for this work must be obedient; they must not jump up on people. They must be confident dogs, not spooked by wheelchairs, crutches, and an assortment of braces, splints and other apparatus. A good start for therapy dog work would be training for the AKC Canine Good Citizen test. This test can be modified for therapy dog work. It is truly gratifying to see how patients open up to dogs, and the dogs used for this work clearly enjoy the attention they receive.

German Shorthairs are beginning to demonstrate their skill as "agility dogs." In the newly created AKC Agility Trials, the

POPpup's™ are healthy treats for your German Shorthaired Pointer. When bone-hard they help to control plaque build-up; when microwaved they become a rich cracker which your GSP will love. The POPpup™ is available in liver and other flavors and is fortified with calcium.

Good training will enable both of you to live life to it's fullest. Ch. Laden Fields Limited Edition, owned by Bruce and Ellen Ladenheim.

handler instructs the dog to negotiate a course consisting of various obstacles, and jumps within an allotted amount of time. The first AKC agility trial was held on August 1, 1994. The AKC offers four levels of agility titles. This is a fun activity for both dog and owner. A well-socialized German Shorthaired Pointer should be able to master the course with success. Many German Shorthaired Pointers have been donated to police departments to be trained for drug detection, and they have also been trained for bomb detection and arson work.

Both hunting tests and obedience trials offer German Shorthair Pointer owners a means of demonstrating their dog's performance skill in hunting and obedience respectively. Neutered and spayed dogs may compete in both.

The satisfaction derived from a trained German Shorthaired Pointer is limitless. It is your investment of time, energy and knowledge that will enhance your German Shorthair's life, and make him all that he is capable of being. Training your dog will create a bond between you and your dog that cannot be expressed in words.

SPORT of Purebred Dogs

Welcome to the exciting and sometimes frustrating sport of dogs. No doubt you are trying to learn more about dogs or you wouldn't be deep into this book. This section covers the basics that may entice you, further your knowledge and help you to understand the dog world.

Dog showing has been a very popular sport for a long time and has been taken quite seriously by some. Others only enjoy it as a hobby.

The Kennel Club in England was formed in 1859, the American Kennel Club was established in 1884 and the Canadian Kennel Club was formed in 1888. The purpose of these clubs was to register purebred dogs and maintain their Stud Books. In the beginning, the concept of registering dogs was not readily accepted. More than 36 million dogs have been enrolled in the AKC Stud Book since its inception in 1888. Presently the kennel clubs not only register dogs but adopt and enforce rules and regulations governing dog shows, obedience trials and field trials. Over the years they have fostered and encouraged interest in the health and welfare of the purebred dog. They routinely donate funds to veterinary research for study on genetic disorders.

Below are the addresses of the kennel clubs in the United States, Great Britain and Canada.

The American Kennel Club
51 Madison Avenue
New York, NY 10010
(Their registry is located at: 5580 Centerview Drive, STE 200, Raleigh, NC 27606-3390)

The Kennel Club
1 Clarges Street
Piccadilly, London, WIY 8AB, England

The Canadian Kennel Club
111 Eglinton Avenue
East Toronto, Ontario M6S 4V7
Canada

Today there are numerous activities that are enjoyable for both the dog and the handler. Some of the activities include conformation showing, obedience competition, tracking, agility, the Canine Good Citizen Certificate, and a wide range of instinct tests that vary from breed to breed. Where you start depends upon your goals which early on may not be readily apparent.

PUPPY KINDERGARTEN

Every puppy will benefit from this class. PKT is the foundation for all future dog activities from conformation to "couch potatoes." Pet owners should make an effort to attend even if they never expect to show their dog. The class is designed for puppies about three

Author Joan Tabor with Ch. Tabor's Reason to Believe.

months of age with graduation at approximately five months of age. All the puppies will be in the same age group and, even though some may be a little unruly, there should not be any real problem. This class will teach the puppy some beginning obedience. As in all obedience classes the owner learns how to train his own dog. The PKT class gives the puppy the opportunity to interact with other puppies in the same age group and exposes him to strangers, which is very important. Some dogs grow up with behavior problems, one of them being fear of strangers. As you can see, there can be much to gain from this class.

There are basic commands that every GSP should know how to perform. Karen Allen with one of her top pupils.

There are some basic obedience exercises that every dog should learn. Some of these can be started with puppy kindergarten.

Sit

One way of teaching the sit is to have your dog on your left side with the leash in your right hand, close to the collar. Pull up on the leash and at the same time reach around his hindlegs with your left hand and tuck them in. As you are doing this say, "Beau, sit." Always use the dog's name when you give an active command. Some owners like to use a treat holding it over the dog's head. The dog will need to sit to get the treat. Encourage the dog to hold the sit for a few seconds, which will eventually be the beginning of the Sit/Stay. Depending on how cooperative he is, you can rub him under the chin or stroke his back. It is a good time to establish eye contact.

Down

Sit the dog on your left side and kneel down beside him with the leash in your right hand. Reach over him with your left hand and grasp his left foreleg. With your right hand, take his right foreleg and pull his legs forward while you say, "Beau, down." If he tries to get up, lean on his shoulder to encourage him to stay down. It will relax your dog if you stroke his back while he is down. Try to encourage him to stay down for a few seconds as preparation for the Down/Stay.

Heel

The definition of heeling is the dog walking under control at your left heel. Your puppy will learn controlled walking in the puppy kindergarten class, which will eventually lead to heeling. The command is "Beau, heel," and you start off briskly with your left foot. Your leash is in your right hand and your left hand is holding it about half way down. Your left hand should be able to control the leash and there should be a little slack in it. You want him to walk with you with your leg somewhere between his nose and his shoulder. You need to encourage him to stay with you, not forging (in front of you) or lagging behind you. It is best to keep him on a fairly short lead. Do not allow the lead to become tight. It is far better to give him a little jerk when necessary and remind him to heel. When you come to a halt, be prepared physically to make him sit. It takes practice to become coordinated. There are excellent books on training that you may wish to purchase. Your instructor should be able to recommend one for you.

Recall

This quite possibly is the most important exercise you will ever teach. It should be a pleasant experience. The puppy may learn to do random recalls while being attached to a long line such as a clothes line. Later the exercise will start with the dog sitting and staying until called. The command is "Beau, come." Let your command be happy. You want your dog to come willingly and faithfully. The recall could save his life if he sneaks out the door. In practicing the recall, let him jump on you or touch you before you reach for him. If he is shy, then kneel down to his level. Reaching for the insecure dog could frighten him, and he may not be willing to come again in the future. Lots of praise and a treat would be in order whenever you do a recall. Under no circumstances should you ever correct your dog when he has come to you. Later in formal obedience your dog will be required to sit in front of you after recalling and then go to heel position.

CONFORMATION

Conformation showing is our oldest dog show sport. This type of showing is based on the dog's appearance—that is his structure, movement and attitude. When considering this type of showing, you need to be aware of your breed's standard and be able to evaluate your dog compared to that standard. The breeder of your puppy or other experienced breeders would be good sources for such an evaluation. Puppies can go through lots of changes over a period of time. Many puppies start out as promising hopefuls and then after maturing may be disappointing as show candidates. Even so this should not deter them from being excellent pets.

In conformation your dog is judged by how closely he conforms to the breed standard. Looks like Ch. Tabor's Conspicuous Consumer is getting an early jump on the competition!

Usually conformation training classes are offered by the local kennel or obedience clubs. These are excellent places for training puppies. The puppy should be able to walk on a lead before entering such a class. Proper ring procedure and technique for posing (stacking) the dog will be demonstrated as well as gaiting the dog. Usually certain patterns are used in the ring such as the triangle or the "L." Conformation class, like the PKT class, will give your youngster the opportunity to socialize with different breeds of dogs and humans too.

It takes some time to learn the routine of conformation showing. Usually one starts at the puppy matches that may be AKC Sanctioned or Fun Matches. These matches are generally for puppies from two or three months to a year old, and there may be classes for the adult over the age of 12 months. Similar to point shows, the classes are divided by sex and after completion of the classes in that breed or variety, the class winners compete for Best of Breed or Variety. The winner goes on to compete in the Group and the Group winners compete for Best in Match. No championship points are awarded for match wins.

A few matches can be great training for puppies even though there is no intention to go on showing. Matches enable the puppy to meet new people and be handled by a stranger—

the judge. It is also a change of environment, which broadens the horizon for both dog and handler. Matches and other dog activities boost the confidence of the handler and especially the younger handlers.

Earning an AKC championship is built on a point system, which is different from Great Britain. To become an AKC Champion of Record the dog must earn 15 points. The number of points earned each time depends upon the number of dogs in competition. The number of points available at each show depends upon the breed, its sex and the location of the show. The United States is divided into ten AKC zones. Each zone has its own set of points. The purpose of the zones is to try to equalize the points available from breed to breed and area to area. The AKC adjusts the point scale annually.

The number of points that can be won at a show are between one and five. Three-, four- and five-point wins are considered majors. Not only does the dog need 15 points won under three different judges, but those points must include two majors under two different judges. Canada also works on a point system but majors are not required.

Dogs always show before bitches. The classes available to those seeking points are: Puppy (which may be divided into 6 to 9 months and 9 to 12 months); 12 to 18 months; Novice; Bred-by-Exhibitor; American-bred; and Open. The class winners of the same sex of each breed or variety compete against each other for Winners Dog and Winners Bitch. A Reserve Winners Dog and Reserve Winners Bitch are also awarded but do not carry any points unless the Winners win is disallowed by AKC. The Winners Dog and Bitch compete with the specials (those dogs that have attained championship) for

Best of Breed or Variety, Best of Winners and Best of Opposite Sex. It is possible to pick up an extra point or even a major if the points are higher for the defeated winner than those of Best of Winners. The latter

Conformation training classes are often offered by local kennels and obedience clubs.

Laden Field's Chief Kamiak owned by B. and E. Ladenheim taking Best of Winners at the Westwind Sporting Dog Club Show.

would get the higher total from the defeated winner.

At an all-breed show, each Best of Breed or Variety winner will go on to his respective Group and then the Group winners will compete against each other for Best in Show. There are seven Groups: Sporting, Hounds, Working, Terriers, Toys, Non-Sporting and Herding. Obviously there are no Groups at speciality shows (those shows that have only one breed or a show such as the American Spaniel Club's Flushing Spaniel Show, which is for all flushing spaniel breeds).

Earning a championship in England is somewhat different since they do not have a point system. Challenge Certificates are awarded if the judge feels the dog is deserving regardless of the number of dogs in competition. A dog must earn three Challenge Certificates under three different judges, with at least one of these Certificates being won after the age of 12 months. Competition is very strong and entries may be higher than they are in the U.S. The Kennel Club's Challenge Certificates are only available at Championship Shows.

In England, The Kennel Club regulations require that certain dogs, Border Collies and Gundog breeds, qualify in a working capacity (i.e., obedience or field trials) before becoming a full Champion. If they do not qualify in the working aspect, then they are designated a Show Champion, which is equivalent to the AKC's Champion of Record. A Gundog may be granted the title of Field Trial Champion (FT Ch.) if it passes all the tests in the field but would also have to qualify in conformation before becoming a full Champion. A Border Collie that earns the title of Obedience Champion (Ob Ch.) must also qualify in the conformation ring before becoming a Champion.

The U.S. doesn't have a designation full Champion but does award for Dual and Triple Champions. The Dual Champion must be a Champion of Record, and either Champion Tracker, Herding Champion, Obedience Trial Champion or Field Champion. Any dog that has been awarded the titles of Champion of Record, and any two of the following: Champion Tracker, Herding Champion, Obedience Trial Champion or Field Champion, may be designated as a Triple Champion.

Handlers must pose their show GSPs in the most flattering position to emphasize the dog's specific strengths.

The shows in England seem to put more emphasis on breeder judges than those in the U.S. There is much competition within the breeds. Therefore the quality of the individual breeds should be very good. In the United States we tend to have more "all around judges" (those that judge multiple breeds) and use the breeder judges at the specialty shows. Breeder judges are more familiar with their own breed since they are actively breeding that breed or did so at one time. Americans emphasize Group and Best in Show wins and promote them accordingly.

The shows in England can be very large and extend over several days, with the Groups being scheduled on different days. Though multi-day shows are not common in the U.S.,

Successful showing requires dedication and preparation, but most of all, it should be an enjoyable experience for handlers and dogs alike.

there are cluster shows, where several different clubs will use the same show site over consecutive days.

Westminster Kennel Club is our most prestigious show although the entry is limited to 2500. In recent years, entry has been limited to Champions. This show is more formal than the majority of the shows with the judges wearing formal attire and the handlers fashionably dressed. In most instances the quality of the dogs is superb. After all, it is a show of Champions. It is a good show to study the AKC registered breeds and is by far the most exciting—especially since it is televised! WKC is one of the few shows in this country that is still benched. This means the dog must be in his benched area during the show hours except when he is being groomed, in the ring, or being exercised.

Typically, the handlers are very particular about their appearances. They are careful not to wear something that will detract from their dog but will perhaps enhance it. American ring procedure is quite formal compared to that of other countries. There is a certain etiquette expected between the judge and exhibitor and among the other exhibitors. Of course it is not always the case but the judge is supposed to be polite, not engaging in small talk or acknowledging how well he knows the handler. There is a more informal and relaxed atmosphere at the shows in other countries. For instance, the dress code is more casual. I can see where this might be more fun for the exhibitor and especially for the novice. The U.S. is very handler-oriented in many of the breeds. It is true, in most instances, that the experienced professional handler can present the dog better and will have a feel for what a judge likes.

Excelling in the show ring is easy for a working dog like the German Shorthaired Pointer who is used to following orders from his master. Ch. Crossing Creeks Homesteader. Owned by Ken and Judy Marden.

In England, Crufts is The Kennel Club's own show and is most assuredly the largest dog show in the world. They've been known to have an entry of nearly 20,000, and the show lasts four days. Entry is only gained by qualifying through winning in specified classes at another Championship Show. Westminster is strictly conformation, but Crufts exhibitors and spectators enjoy not only conformation but obedience, agility and a multitude of exhibitions as well. Obedience was admitted in 1957 and agility in 1983.

If you are handling your own dog, please give some consideration to your apparel. For sure the dress code at matches is more informal than the point shows. However, you should wear something a little more appropriate than beach attire or ragged jeans and bare feet. If you check out the handlers and see what is presently fashionable, you'll catch on. Men usually dress with a shirt and tie and a nice sports coat. Whether you

Handlers must wear comfortable practical clothing that does not distract attention from the dog they are showing.

Ch. Tabor's Zephyr of Orion owned by Joan and Joel Tabor.

are male or female, you will want to wear comfortable clothes and shoes. You need to be able to run with your dog and you certainly don't want to take a chance of falling and hurting yourself. Heaven forbid, if nothing else, you'll upset your dog. Women usually wear a dress or two-piece outfit, preferably with pockets to carry bait, comb, brush, etc. In this case men are the lucky ones with all their pockets. Ladies, think about where your dress will be if you need to kneel on the floor and also think about running. Does it allow freedom to do so?

You need to take along dog; crate; ex pen (if you use one); extra newspaper; water pail and water; all required grooming equipment, including hair dryer and extension cord; table; chair for you; bait for dog and lunch for you and friends; and, last but not least, clean up materials, such as plastic bags, paper towels, and perhaps a bath towel and some shampoo— just in case. Don't forget your entry confirmation and directions to the show.

If you are showing in obedience, then you will want to wear pants. Many of our top obedience handlers wear pants that are color-coordinated with their dogs. The philosophy is that imperfections in the black dog will be less obvious next to your black pants.

Whether you are showing in conformation, Junior Showmanship or obedience, you need to watch the clock and be sure you are not late. It is customary to pick up your conformation armband a few minutes before the start of the class. They will not wait for you and if you are on the show grounds and not in the ring, you will upset everyone. It's a little more complicated picking up your obedience armband if you show later in the class. If you have not picked up your armband and they get to your number, you may not be allowed to show. It's best to pick up your armband early, but then you may show earlier than expected if other handlers don't pick up. Customarily all conflicts should be discussed with the judge prior to the start of the class.

Training for any type of competition allows the owner and his dog to develop closeness through working together.

Junior Showmanship

The Junior Showmanship Class is a wonderful way to build self confidence even if there are no aspirations of staying with the dog-show game later in life. Frequently, Junior Showmanship becomes the background of those who become successful exhibitors/handlers in the future. In some instances it is taken very seriously, and success is measured in terms of wins. The Junior Handler is judged solely on his ability and skill in presenting his dog. The dog's conformation is not to be considered by the judge. Even so the condition and grooming of the dog may be a reflection upon the handler.

Usually the matches and point shows include different classes. The Junior Handler's dog may be entered in a breed or obedience class and even shown by another person in that class. Junior Showmanship classes are usually divided by age and perhaps sex. The age is determined by the handler's age on the day of the show. The classes are:

Novice Junior for those at least ten and under 14 years of age who at time of entry closing have not won three first places in a Novice Class at a licensed or member show.

Novice Senior for those at least 14 and under 18 years of age who at the time of entry closing have not won three first places in a Novice Class at a licensed or member show.

Open Junior for those at least ten and under 14 years of age who at the time of entry closing have won at least three first places in a Novice Junior Showmanship Class at a licensed or member show with competition present.

Open Senior for those at least 14 and under 18 years of age who at time of entry closing have won at least three first places in a Novice Junior Showmanship Class at a licensed or member show with competition present.

Junior Handlers must include their AKC Junior Handler number on each show entry. This needs to be obtained from the AKC.

CANINE GOOD CITIZEN

The AKC sponsors a program to encourage dog owners to train their dogs. Local clubs perform the pass/fail tests, and dogs who pass are awarded a Canine Good Citizen Certificate. Proof of vaccination is required at the time of participation. The test includes:

Well-trained GSP's can accompany you anywhere. This father and son team await the next command from their master.

1. Accepting a friendly stranger.
2. Sitting politely for petting.
3. Appearance and grooming.
4. Walking on a loose leash.
5. Walking through a crowd.
6. Sit and down on command/staying in place.
7. Come when called.
8. Reaction to another dog.
9. Reactions to distractions.
10. Supervised separation.

If more effort was made by pet owners to accomplish these exercises, fewer dogs would be cast off to the humane shelter.

OBEDIENCE

Obedience is necessary, without a doubt, but it can also become a wonderful hobby or even an obsession. Obedience classes and competition can provide wonderful companionship, not only with your dog but with your classmates or fellow competitors. It is always gratifying to discuss your dog's problems with others who have had similar experiences. The AKC acknowledged Obedience around 1936, and it has changed tremendously even though many of the exercises are basically the same. Today, obedience competition is just that—very competitive. Even so, it is possible for every obedience exhibitor to come home a winner (by earning qualifying scores) even though he/she may not earn a placement in the class.

Most of the obedience titles are awarded after earning three qualifying scores (legs) in the appropriate class under three

different judges. These classes offer a perfect score of 200, which is extremely rare. Each of the class exercises has its own point value. A leg is earned after receiving a score of at least 170 and at least 50 percent of the points available in each exercise. The titles are:

Ch. Tabor's You Wear It Well JH, owned by F. & L. Del Prete, is an example of a well-mannered house pet.

103

Companion Dog–CD

This is called the Novice Class and the exercises are:

1. Heel on leash and figure 8	40 points
2. Stand for examination	30 points
3. Heel free	40 points
4. Recall	30 points
5. Long sit—one minute	30 points
6. Long down—three minutes	30 points
Maximum total score	200 points

Companion Dog Excellent–CDX

This is the Open Class and the exercises are:

1. Heel off leash and figure 8	40 points
2. Drop on recall	30 points
3. Retrieve on flat	20 points
4. Retrieve over high jump	30 points
5. Broad jump	20 points
6. Long sit—three minutes (out of sight)	30 points
7. Long down—five minutes (out of sight)	30 points
Maximum total score	200 points

Utility Dog–UD

The Utility Class exercises are:

1. Signal Exercise	40 points
2. Scent discrimination-Article 1	30 points
3. Scent discrimination-Article 2	30 points
4. Directed retrieve	30 points
5. Moving stand and examination	30 points
6. Directed jumping	40 points
Maximum total score	200 points

After achieving the UD title, you may feel inclined to go after the UDX and/or OTCh. The UDX (Utility Dog Excellent) title went into effect in January 1994. It is not easily attained. The title requires qualifying simultaneously ten times in Open B and Utility B but not necessarily at consecutive shows.

The OTCh (Obedience Trial Champion) is awarded after the dog has earned his UD and then goes on to earn 100 championship points, a first place in Utility, a first place in Open and another first place in either class. The placements must be won under three different judges at all-breed obedience trials. The points are determined by the number of dogs competing in the Open B and Utility B classes. The OTCh title precedes the dog's name.

German Shorthaired Pointers excel in scenting exercises because of their natural ability to use their noses.

Obedience matches (AKC Sanctioned, Fun, and Show and Go) are usually available. Usually they are sponsored by the local obedience clubs. When preparing an obedience dog for a title, you will find matches very helpful. Fun Matches and Show and Go Matches are more lenient in allowing you to make corrections in the ring. This type of training is usually very necessary for the Open and Utility Classes. AKC Sanctioned Obedience Matches do not allow corrections in the ring since they

Agility competition is growing in popularity. Ch. Sunreach's Flexible Flyer, CDX, CGC, easily clears a jump.

must abide by the AKC Obedience Regulations. If you are interested in showing in obedience, then you should contact the AKC for a copy of the Obedience Regulations.

AGILITY

Agility was first introduced by John Varley in England at the Crufts Dog Show, February 1978, but Peter Meanwell, competitor and judge, actually developed the idea. It was officially recognized in the early '80s. Agility is extremely popular in England and Canada and growing in popularity in the U.S. The AKC acknowledged agility in August 1994. Dogs must be at least 12 months of age to be entered. It is a fascinating sport that the dog, handler and spectators enjoy to the utmost. Agility is a spectator sport! The dog performs off lead. The handler either runs with his dog or positions himself on the course and directs his dog with verbal and hand signals over a timed course over or through a variety of obstacles including a time out or pause. One of the main drawbacks to agility is finding a place to train. The obstacles take up a lot of space and it is very time consuming to put up and take down courses.

The titles earned at AKC agility trials are Novice Agility Dog (NAD), Open Agility Dog (OAD), Agility Dog Excellent (ADX), and Master Agility Excellent (MAX). In order to acquire an agility title, a dog must earn a qualifying score in its respective class on three separate occasions under two different judges. The MAX will be awarded after earning ten qualifying scores in the Agility Excellent Class.

PERFORMANCE TESTS

During the last decade the American Kennel Club has promoted performance tests–those events that test the different breeds' natural abilities. This type of event encourages a handler to devote even more time to his dog and retain the natural instincts of his breed heritage. It is an important part of the wonderful world of dogs.

Hunting Titles

For retrievers, pointing breeds and spaniels. Titles offered are Junior Hunter (JH), Senior Hunter (SH), and Master Hunter (MH).

Flushing Spaniels Their primary purpose is to hunt, find, flush and return birds to hand as quickly as possible in a pleasing and obedient manner. The entrant must be at least six months of age and dogs with limited registration (ILP) are eligible. Game used are pigeons, pheasants, and quail.

Retrievers Limited registration (ILP) retrievers are not eligible to compete in Hunting Tests. The purpose of a Hunting Test for retrievers is to test the merits of and evaluate the abilities of retrievers in the field in order to determine their suitability and ability as hunting companions. They are expected to retrieve any type of game bird, pheasants, ducks, pigeons, guinea hens and quail.

Because of their extensive background in fieldwork, the German Shorthaired Pointer does very well in tracking competitions.

Pointing Breeds Are eligible at six months of age, and dogs with limited registration (ILP) are permitted. They must show a keen desire to hunt; be bold and independent; have a fast, yet attractive, manner of hunting; and demonstrate intelligence not only in seeking objectives but also in the ability to find game. They must establish point, and in the more advanced tests they need to be steady to wing and must remain in position until the bird is shot or they are released.

A Senior Hunter must retrieve. A Master Hunter must honor. The judges and the marshal are permitted to ride horseback during the test, but all handling must be done on foot.

Obedience trial and tracking test information is available through the AKC. Frequently these events are not superintended, but put on by the host club. Therefore you would make the entry with the event's secretary.

As you have read, there are numerous activities you can share with your dog. Regardless what you do, it does take teamwork. Your dog can only benefit from your attention and training. We hope this chapter has enlightened you and hope, if nothing else, you will attend a show here and there. Perhaps you will start with a puppy kindergarten class, and who knows where it may lead!

HEALTH CARE

Veterinary medicine has become far more sophisticated than what was available to our ancestors. This can be attributed to the increase in household pets and consequently the demand for better care for them. Also human medicine has become far more complex. Today diagnostic testing in veterinary medicine parallels human diagnostics. Because of better technology we can expect our pets to live healthier lives thereby increasing their life spans.

THE FIRST CHECK UP

You will want to take your new puppy/dog in for its first check up within 48 to 72 hours after acquiring it. Many breeders strongly recommend this check up and so do the humane shelters. A puppy/dog can appear healthy but it may have a serious problem that is not apparent to the layman. Most pets have some type of a minor flaw that may never cause a real problem.

For the sake of your puppy as well as the health of your family, you should bring your new GSP to the veterinarian within three days of his arrival at your home.

Unfortunately if he/she should have a serious problem, you will want to consider the consequences of keeping the pet and the attachments that will be formed, which may be broken prematurely. Keep in mind there are many healthy dogs looking for good homes.

This first check up is a good time to establish yourself with the veterinarian and learn the office policy regarding their hours and how they handle emergencies. Usually the breeder or another conscientious pet owner is a good reference for locating a capable veterinarian. You should be aware that not all veterinarians give the same quality of service. Please do not make your selection on the least expensive clinic, as they may be short changing your pet. There is the possibility that eventually it will cost you more due to improper diagnosis, treatment, etc. If you are selecting a new veterinarian, feel free to ask for a tour of the clinic. You should inquire about

making an appointment for a tour since all clinics are working clinics, and therefore may not be available all day for sightseers. You may worry less if you see where your pet will be spending the day if he ever needs to be hospitalized.

THE PHYSICAL EXAM

Your veterinarian will check your pet's overall condition, which includes listening to the heart; checking the respiration; feeling the abdomen, muscles and joints; checking the mouth, which includes the gum color and signs of gum disease along with plaque buildup; checking the ears for signs of an infection or ear mites; examining the eyes; and, last but not least, checking the condition of the skin and coat.

He should ask you questions regarding your pet's eating and elimination habits and invite you to relay your questions. It is a good idea to prepare a list so as not to forget anything. He should discuss the proper diet and the quantity to be fed. If this should differ from your breeder's recommendation, then you should convey to him the breeder's choice and see if he approves. If he recommends changing the diet, then this should be done over a few days so as not to cause a gastrointestinal upset. It is customary to take in a fresh stool sample (just a small amount) for a test for intestinal parasites. It must be fresh, preferably within 12 hours, since the eggs hatch quickly and after hatching will not be observed under the microscope. If your pet isn't obliging then, usually the technician can take one in the clinic.

IMMUNIZATIONS

It is important that you take your puppy/dog's vaccination record with you on your first visit. In case of a puppy, presumably the breeder has seen to the vaccinations up to the time you acquired custody. Veterinarians differ in their vaccination protocol. It is not unusual for your puppy to have received vaccinations for distemper, hepatitis, leptospirosis, parvovirus and parainfluenza every two to three weeks from the age of five or six weeks. Usually this is a combined injection and is typically called the DHLPP. The DHLPP is given through at least 12 to 14 weeks of age, and it is customary to continue with another parvovirus vaccine at 16 to 18 weeks. You may wonder why so many immunizations are necessary.

No one knows for sure when the puppy's maternal antibodies are gone, although it is customarily accepted that distemper antibodies are gone by 12 weeks. Usually parvovirus antibodies are gone by 16 to 18 weeks of age. However, it is possible for the maternal antibodies to be gone at a much earlier age or even a later age. Therefore immunizations are started at an early age. The vaccine will not give immunity as long as there are maternal antibodies.

The rabies vaccination is given at three or six months of age depending on your local laws. A vaccine for bordetella (kennel cough) is advisable and can be given anytime from the age of five weeks. The coronavirus is not commonly given unless there is a problem locally. The Lyme vaccine is necessary in endemic areas. Lyme disease has been reported in 47 states.

Through breeding dogs that are only of the best quality we are assured that good health and temperament will be passed down to each new generation.

Distemper

This is virtually an incurable disease. If the dog recovers, he is subject to severe nervous disorders. The virus attacks every tissue in the body and resembles a bad cold with a fever. It can cause

a runny nose and eyes and cause gastrointestinal disorders, including a poor appetite, vomiting and diarrhea. The virus is carried by raccoons, foxes, wolves, mink and other dogs. Unvaccinated youngsters and senior citizens are very susceptible. This is still a common disease.

Hepatitis

This is a virus that is most serious in very young dogs. It is spread by contact with an infected animal or its stool or urine. The virus affects the liver and kidneys and is characterized by high fever, depression and lack of appetite. Recovered animals may be afflicted with chronic illnesses.

Leptospirosis

This is a bacterial disease transmitted by contact with the urine of an infected dog, rat or other wildlife. It produces severe symptoms of fever, depression, jaundice and internal bleeding and was fatal before the vaccine was developed. Recovered dogs can be carriers, and the disease can be transmitted from dogs to humans.

Parvovirus

This was first noted in the late 1970s and is still a fatal disease. However, with proper vaccinations, early diagnosis

and prompt treatment, it is a manageable disease. It attacks the bone marrow and intestinal tract. The symptoms include depression, loss of appetite, vomiting, diarrhea and collapse. Immediate medical attention is of the essence.

Rabies

This is shed in the saliva and is carried by raccoons, skunks, foxes, other dogs

A healthy and tasty treat for your German Shorthaired Pointer because they love cheese is CHOOZ™. CHOOZ™ are bone-hard but can be microwaved to expand into a huge, crispy dog biscuit. They are almost fat free and about 70% protein.

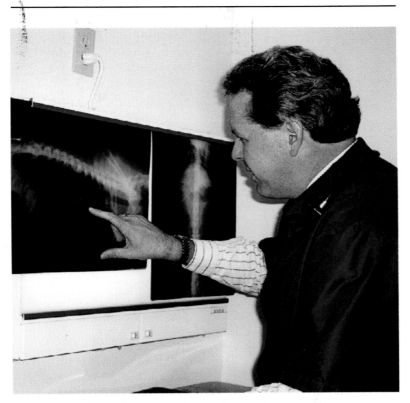

Regular visits to the veterinarian will help in the timely diagnosis of any illnesses.

and cats. It attacks nerve tissue, resulting in paralysis and death. Rabies can be transmitted to people and is virtually always fatal. This disease is reappearing in the suburbs.

Bordetella (Kennel Cough)

The symptoms are coughing, sneezing, hacking and retching accompanied by nasal discharge usually lasting from a few days to several weeks. There are several disease-producing organisms responsible for this disease. The present vaccines are helpful but do not protect for all the strains. It usually is not life threatening but in some instances it can progress to a serious bronchopneumonia. The disease is highly contagious. The vaccination should be given routinely for dogs that come in contact with other dogs, such as through boarding, training class or visits to the groomer.

113

Regular medical care is just as important for the adult GSP as it is for the puppy. Vaccination boosters and physical exams are part of your dog's lifelong maintenance.

Coronavirus

This is usually self limiting and not life threatening. It was first noted in the late '70s about a year before parvovirus. The virus produces a yellow/brown stool and there may be depression, vomiting and diarrhea.

Lyme Disease

This was first diagnosed in the United States in 1976 in Lyme, CT in people who lived in close proximity to the deer tick. Symptoms may include acute lameness, fever, swelling of joints and loss of appetite. Your veterinarian can advise you if you live in an endemic area.

After your puppy has completed his puppy vaccinations, you will continue to booster the DHLPP once a year. It is customary to booster the rabies one year after the first vaccine and then, depending on where you live, it should be boostered every year or every three years. This depends on your local laws. The Lyme and corona vaccines are boostered annually and it is recommended that the bordetella be boostered every six to eight months.

I would like to impress the importance of the annual check up, which would include the booster vaccinations, check for intestinal parasites and test for heartworm. Today in our very busy world it is rush, rush and see "how much you can get for how little." Unbelievably, some non-veterinary businesses have entered into the vaccination business. More harm than good can come to your dog through improper vaccinations, possibly from inferior vaccines and/or the wrong schedule. More than likely

Laboratory tests are studied by highly trained veterinary technicians. Most tests are performed right in your own veterinarian's office.

you truly care about your companion dog and over the years you have devoted much time and expense to his well being. Perhaps you are unaware that a vaccination is not just a vaccination. There is more involved. Please, please follow through with regular physical examinations.

It is so important for your veterinarian to know your dog and this is especially true during middle age through the geriatric years. More than likely your older dog will require more than one physical a year. The annual physical is good preventive medicine. Through early diagnosis and subsequent treatment your dog can maintain a longer and better quality of life.

INTESTINAL PARASITES

Hookworms

These are almost microscopic intestinal worms that can cause anemia and therefore serious problems, including death, in young puppies. Hookworms can be transmitted to humans through penetration of the skin. Puppies may be born with them.

Roundworms

These are spaghetti-like worms that can cause a potbellied appearance and dull coat along with more severe symptoms, such as vomiting, diarrhea and coughing. Puppies acquire these while in the mother's uterus and through lactation. Both hookworms and roundworms may be acquired through ingestion.

Whipworms

These have a three-month life cycle and are not acquired through the dam. They cause intermittent diarrhea usually with mucus. Whipworms are possibly the most difficult worm to eradicate. Their eggs are very resistant to most environmental factors and can last for years until the proper conditions enable them to mature. Whipworms are seldom seen in the stool.

Whipworms are hard to detect, and it is a job best left to a veterinarian. Pictured here are adult whipworms.

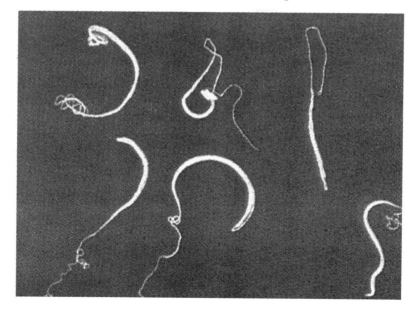

The GSP is an active dog that should be energetic and alert. Any changes in his activity should be brought to your veterinarian's attention immediately.

Intestinal parasites are more prevalent in some areas than others. Climate, soil and contamination are big factors contributing to the incidence of intestinal parasites. Eggs are passed in the stool, lay on the ground and then become infective in a certain number of days. Each of the above worms has a different life cycle. Your best chance of becoming and remaining worm-free is to always pooper-scoop your yard. A fenced-in yard keeps stray dogs out, which is certainly helpful.

I would recommend having a fecal examination on your dog twice a year or more often if there is a problem. If your dog has a positive fecal sample, then he will be given the appropriate medication and you will be asked to bring back another stool sample in a certain period of time (depending on the type of worm) and then be rewormed. This process goes on until he has at least two negative samples. The different types of worms require different medications. You will be wasting your money and doing your dog an injustice by buying over-the-counter medication without first consulting your veterinarian.

OTHER INTERNAL PARASITES

Coccidiosis and Giardiasis
These protozoal infections usually affect puppies, especially in places where large numbers of puppies are brought together. Older dogs may harbor these infections but do not show signs unless they are stressed. Symptoms include diarrhea, weight loss and lack of appetite. These infections are not always apparent in the fecal examination.

Tapeworms
Seldom apparent on fecal floatation, they are diagnosed frequently as rice-like segments around the dog's anus and the base of the tail. Tapeworms are long, flat and ribbon like, sometimes several feet in length, and made up of many segments about five-eighths of an inch long. The two most common types of tapeworms found in the dog are:
(1) First the larval form of the flea tapeworm parasite must mature in an intermediate host, the flea, before it can become infective. Your dog acquires this by ingesting the flea through licking and chewing.
(2) Rabbits, rodents and certain large game animals serve as

intermediate hosts for other species of tapeworms. If your dog should eat one of these infected hosts, then he can acquire tapeworms.

HEARTWORM DISEASE
This is a worm that resides in the heart and adjacent blood vessels of the lung that produces microfilaria,

Dirofilaria— adult worms in the heart of a dog. Courtesy of Merck Ag Vet.

The cat flea is the most common flea of both dogs and cats. It starts feeding soon after it makes contact with the dog.

which circulate in the bloodstream. It is possible for a dog to be infected with any number of worms from one to a hundred that can be 6 to 14 inches long. It is a life-threatening disease, expensive to treat and easily prevented. Depending on where you live, your veterinarian may recommend a preventive year-round and either an annual or semiannual blood test. The most common preventive is given once a month.

EXTERNAL PARASITES

Fleas

These pests are not only the dog's worst enemy but also enemy to the owner's pocketbook. Preventing is less expensive than treating, but regardless we'd prefer to spend our money elsewhere. Likely, the majority of our dogs are allergic to the bite of a flea, and in many cases it only takes one flea bite. The protein in the flea's saliva is the culprit. Allergic dogs have a reaction, which usually results in a "hot spot." More than likely such a reaction will involve a trip to the veterinarian for treatment. Yes, prevention is less expensive. Fortunately today there are several good products available.

If there is a flea infestation, no one product is going to correct the problem. Not only will the dog require treatment so will the environment. In general flea collars are not very effective although there is now available an "egg" collar that will kill the eggs on the dog. Dips are the most economical but they are messy. There are some effective shampoos and treatments available through pet shops and veterinarians. An oral tablet arrived on the American market in 1995 and was popular in Europe the previous year. It sterilizes the female flea but will not kill adult fleas. Therefore the tablet, which is given monthly, will decrease the flea population but is not a "cure-all." Those dogs that suffer from flea-bite allergy will still be subjected to the bite of the flea. Another popular parasiticide is permethrin, which is applied to the back of the dog in one or two places depending on the dog's weight. This product works as a repellent causing the flea to get "hot feet" and jump off. Do not confuse this product with some of the organophosphates that are also applied to the dog's back.

Some products are not usable on young puppies. Treating fleas should be done under your veterinarian's guidance. Frequently it is necessary to combine products and the layman does not have the knowledge regarding possible toxicities. It is hard to believe but there are a few dogs that do have a natural resistance to fleas. Nevertheless it would be wise to treat all pets at the same time. Don't forget your cats. Cats just love to prowl the neighborhood and consequently return with unwanted guests.

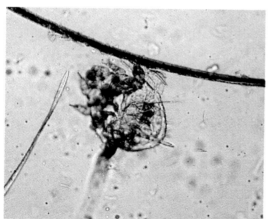

Sarcoptic mange is highly contagious to other dogs as well as humans. Sarcoptes cause intense itching.

Adult fleas live on the dog but their eggs drop off the dog into the environment. There they go through four larval stages before reaching adulthood, and thereby are able to jump back on the poor unsuspecting dog. The cycle resumes and takes between 21 to 28 days under ideal conditions. There are environmental products available that will kill both the adult fleas and the larvae.

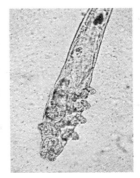

Demodectic mange is passed from a dam to her puppies. It involves areas of hair loss.

Ticks

Ticks carry Rocky Mountain Spotted Fever, Lyme disease and can cause tick paralysis. They should be removed with tweezers, trying to pull out the head. The jaws carry disease. There is a tick preventive collar that does an excellent job. The ticks automatically back out on those dogs wearing collars.

Sarcoptic Mange

This is a mite that is difficult to find on skin scrapings. The pinnal reflex is a good indicator of this disease. Rub the ends of the pinna (ear) together and the dog will start scratching with his foot. Sarcoptes are highly contagious to other dogs and to humans although they do not live long on humans. They cause intense itching.

Demodectic Mange

This is a mite that is passed from the dam to her puppies. It affects youngsters age three to ten months. Diagnosis is confirmed by skin scraping. Small areas of alopecia around the eyes, lips and/or forelegs become visible. There is little itching unless there is a secondary bacterial infection. Some breeds are afflicted more than others.

Cheyletiella

This causes intense itching and is diagnosed by skin scraping. It lives in the outer layers of the skin of dogs, cats, rabbits and humans. Yellow-gray scales may be found on the back and the rump, top of the head and the nose.

TO BREED OR NOT TO BREED

More than likely your breeder has requested that you have your puppy neutered or spayed. Your breeder's request is based on what is healthiest for your dog and what is most beneficial for your breed. Experienced and conscientious breeders devote many years into developing a bloodline. In order to do this, he makes every effort to plan each breeding in regard to conformation, temperament and health. This type of breeder does his best to perform the necessary testing (i.e., OFA, CERF, testing for inherited blood disorders, thyroid, etc.). Testing is expensive and sometimes very disheartening when a favorite dog doesn't pass his health tests. The

Breeding should be attempted only by someone who is conscientious, knowledgeable, and willing to take responsibility for the dogs and new puppies involved.

health history pertains not only to the breeding stock but to the immediate ancestors. Reputable breeders do not want their offspring to be bred indiscriminately. Therefore you may be asked to neuter or spay your puppy. Of course there is always the exception, and your breeder may agree to let you breed your dog under his direct supervision. This is an important concept. More and more effort is being made to breed healthier dogs.

Spay/Neuter

There are numerous benefits of performing this surgery at six months of age. Unspayed females are subject to mammary and ovarian cancer. In order to prevent mammary cancer she must be spayed prior to her first heat cycle. Later in life, an unspayed female may develop a pyometra (an infected uterus), which is definitely life threatening.

Spaying is performed under a general anesthetic and is easy on the young dog. As you might expect it is a little harder on the older dog, but that is no reason to deny her the surgery. The surgery removes the ovaries and uterus. It is important to remove all the ovarian tissue. If some is left behind, she could remain attractive to males. In order to view the ovaries, a reasonably long incision is necessary. An ovariohysterectomy is considered major surgery.

Neutering the male at a young age will inhibit some characteristic male behavior that owners frown upon. Some

boys will not hike their legs and mark territory if they are neutered at six months of age. Also neutering at a young age has hormonal benefits, lessening the chance of hormonal aggressiveness.

Surgery involves removing the testicles but leaving the scrotum. If there should be a retained testicle, then he definitely needs to be neutered before the age of two or three years. Retained testicles can develop into cancer. Unneutered

Spaying/neutering is often the best option for your family pet. The health benefits are numerous and it will minimize the risk of certain diseases.

males are at risk for testicular cancer, perineal fistulas, perianal tumors and fistulas and prostatic disease.

Intact males and females are prone to housebreaking accidents. Females urinate frequently before, during and after heat cycles, and males tend to mark territory if there is a female in heat. Males may show the same behavior if there is a visiting dog or guests.

Surgery involves a sterile operating procedure equivalent to human surgery. The incision site is shaved, surgically scrubbed and draped. The veterinarian wears a sterile surgical gown, cap, mask and gloves. Anesthesia should be monitored by a registered technician. It is customary for the veterinarian to recommend a pre-anesthetic blood screening, looking for metabolic problems and a ECG rhythm strip to check for normal heart function. Today anesthetics are equal to human anesthetics, which enables your dog to walk out of the clinic the same day as surgery.

Some folks worry about their dog gaining weight after being neutered or spayed. This is usually not the case. It is true that some dogs may be less active so they could develop a problem, but most dogs are just as active as they were before surgery. However, if your dog should begin to gain, then you need to decrease his food and see to it that he gets a little more exercise.

All German Shorthaired Pointer puppies are cute, but not all are of breeding quality. Reputable breeders will often sell pet-quality pups on the condition that they are spayed or neutered.

DENTAL CARE for Your Dog's Life

So you've got a new puppy! You also have a new set of puppy teeth in your household. Anyone who has ever raised a puppy is abundantly aware of these new teeth. Your puppy will chew anything it can reach, chase your shoelaces, and play "tear the rag" with any piece of clothing it can find. When puppies are newly born, they have no teeth. At about four weeks of age, puppies of most breeds begin to develop their deciduous or baby teeth. They begin eating semi-solid food, fighting and biting with their litter mates, and learning discipline from their mother. As their new teeth come in, they inflict more pain on their mother's breasts, so her feeding sessions become less frequent and shorter. By six or eight weeks, the mother will start growling to warn her pups when they are fighting too roughly or hurting her as they nurse too much with their new teeth.

Puppies need to chew. It is a necessary part of their physical and mental development. They develop muscles and necessary life

Raised dental tips on the surface of every PLAQUE ATTACKER™ bone help to combat plaque and tartar. Safe for aggressive chewers and ruggedly constructed to last, PLAQUE ATTACKER™ dental bones provide hours and hours of tooth-saving enjoyment.

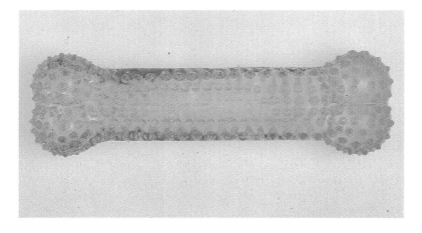

skills as they drag objects around, fight over possession, and vocalize alerts and warnings. Puppies chew on things to explore their world. They are using their sense of taste to determine what is food and what is not. How else can they tell an electrical cord from a lizard? At about four months of age, most puppies begin shedding their baby teeth. Often these teeth need some help to come out and make way for the permanent teeth. The incisors (front teeth) will be replaced first. Then, the adult canine or fang teeth erupt. When the baby tooth is not shed before the permanent tooth comes in, veterinarians call it a retained deciduous tooth. This condition will often cause gum infections by trapping hair and debris between the permanent tooth and the retained baby tooth. Nylafloss® is an excellent device for puppies to use. They can toss it, drag it, and chew on the many surfaces it presents. The baby teeth can catch in the nylon material, aiding in their removal. Puppies that have adequate chew toys will have less destructive behavior, develop more physically, and have less chance of retained deciduous teeth.

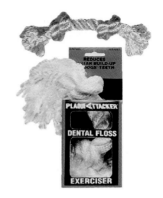

There is only one material suitable for flossing human teeth and that's nylon. So why not get a chew toy that will enable you to interact with your German Shorthaired Pointer while it promotes dental health. As you play tug-o-war with a NYLAFLOSS™, you'll be slowly pulling the nylon strands through your dog's teeth.

During the first year, your dog should be seen by your veterinarian at regular intervals. Your veterinarian will let you know when to bring in your puppy for vaccinations and parasite examinations. At each visit, your veterinarian should inspect the lips, teeth, and mouth as part of a complete physical examination. You should take some part in the maintenance of your dog's oral health. You should examine your dog's mouth weekly throughout his first year to make sure there are no sores, foreign objects, tooth problems, etc. If your dog drools excessively, shakes its head, or has bad

breath, consult your veterinarian. By the time your dog is six months old, the permanent teeth are all in and plaque can start to accumulate on the tooth surfaces. This is when your dog needs to develop good dental-care habits to prevent calculus build-up on its teeth. Brushing is best. That is a fact that cannot be denied. However, some dogs do not like their teeth brushed regularly, or you may not be able to accomplish the task. In that case, you should consider a product that will help prevent plaque and calculus build-up.

Brushing your dog's teeth is recommended by every veterinarian. Use the 2-BRUSH™ regularly, three to four times per week and you may never need your veterinarian to do the job for you.

The Plaque Attackers® and Galileo Bone® are other excellent choices for the first three years of a dog's life. Their shapes make them interesting for the dog. As the dog chews on them, the solid polyurethane massages the gums which improves the blood circulation to the periodontal tissues. Projections on the chew devices increase the surface and are in contact with the tooth for more efficient cleaning. The unique shape and consistency prevent your dog from exerting excessive force on his own teeth or from breaking off pieces of the bone. If your dog is an aggressive chewer or weighs more than 55 pounds (25 kg), you should consider giving him a Nylabone®, the most durable chew product on the market.

The Gumabones ®, made by the Nylabone Company, is constructed of strong polyurethane, which is softer than nylon. Less powerful chewers prefer the Gumabones® to the Nylabones®. A super option for your dog is the Hercules Bone®, a uniquely shaped bone named after the great Olympian for its exception strength. Like all Nylabone products, they are specially scented to make them

If your German Shorthaired Pointer would rather chew than do anything else, the Gumabone™ is for him. Offer him a Gumabone™ made of non-toxic, durable polyurethane to sink his teeth into.

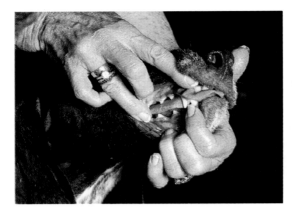

A thorough examination of your German Shorthaired Pointer's mouth, teeth, and gums should be part of his annual check-up.

attractive to your dog. Ask your veterinarian about these bones and he will validate the good doctor's prescription: Nylabones® not only give your dog a good chewing workout but also help to save your dog's teeth (and even his life, as it protects him from possible fatal periodontal diseases).

By the time dogs are four years old, 75% of them have periodontal disease. It is the most common infection in dogs. Yearly examinations by your veterinarian are essential to maintaining your dog's good health. If your veterinarian detects periodontal disease, he or she may recommend a prophylactic cleaning. To do a thorough cleaning, it will be necessary to put your dog under anesthesia. With modern gas anesthetics and monitoring equipment, the procedure is pretty safe. Your veterinarian will scale the teeth with an ultrasound scaler or hand instrument. This removes the calculus from the teeth. If there are calculus deposits below the gum line, the veterinarian will plane the roots to make them smooth. After all of the calculus has been removed, the teeth are polished with pumice in a polishing cup. If any medical or surgical treatment is needed, it is done at this time. The final step would be fluoride treatment and your follow-up treatment at home. If the periodontal disease is advanced, the veterinarian may prescribe a medicated mouth rinse or antibiotics for use at home. Make sure your dog has safe, clean and attractive chew toys and treats. Chooz® treats are another way of using a consumable treat to help keep your dog's teeth clean.

Rawhide is the most popular of all materials for a dog to chew. This has never been good news to dog owners, because rawhide is inherently very dangerous for dogs. Thousands of dogs have died from rawhide, having swallowed the hide after it has become soft and mushy, only to cause stomach and intestinal blockage. A new rawhide product on the market has finally solved the problem of rawhide: molded Roar-Hide® from Nylabone. These are composed of processed, cut up, and melted American rawhide injected into your dog's favorite shape: a dog bone. These dog-safe devices smell and taste like rawhide but don't break up. The ridges on the bones help to fight tartar build-up on the teeth and they last ten times longer than the usual rawhide chews.

As your dog ages, professional examination and cleaning should become more frequent. The mouth should be inspected at least once a year. Your veterinarian may recommend visits every six months. In the geriatric patient, organs such as the heart, liver, and kidneys do not function as well as when they were young. Your veterinarian will probably want to test these organs' functions prior to using general anesthesia for dental cleaning. If your dog is a good chewer and you work closely with your veterinarian, your dog can keep all of its teeth all of its life. However, as your dog ages, his sense of smell, sight, and taste will diminish. He may not have the desire to chase, trap or chew his toys. He will also not have the energy to chew for long periods, as arthritis and periodontal disease make chewing painful. This will leave you with more responsibility for keeping his teeth clean and healthy. The dog that would not let you brush his teeth at one year of age, may let you brush his teeth now that he is ten years old.

If you train your dog with good chewing habits as a puppy, he will have healthier teeth throughout his life.

*There are all kinds of flying disks for dogs, but only one is made with strength, scent, and originality. The Nylabone® Frisbee™ is a must if you want to have this sort of fun with your German Shorthaired Pointer. *The trademark Frisbee is used under license from Mattel, Inc., California, USA.*

TRAVELING with Your Dog

The earlier you start traveling with your new puppy or dog, the better. He needs to become accustomed to traveling. However, some dogs are nervous riders and become carsick easily. It is helpful if he starts with an empty stomach. Do not despair, as it will go better if you continue taking him with you on short fun rides. How would you feel if every time you rode in the car you stopped at the doctor's for an injection? You would soon dread that nasty car. Older dogs that tend to get carsick may have more of a problem adjusting to traveling. Those dogs that are having a serious problem may benefit from some medication prescribed by the veterinarian.

Do give your dog a chance to relieve himself before getting into the car. It is a good idea to be prepared for a clean up with a leash, paper towels, bag and terry cloth towel.

The safest place for your dog is in a fiberglass crate, although close confinement can promote carsickness in some dogs. If your dog is nervous you can try letting him ride on the seat next to you or in someone's lap.

An alternative to the crate would be to use a car harness made for dogs and/or a safety strap attached to the harness or collar. Whatever you do, do not let your dog ride in the back of a pickup truck unless he is securely tied on a very short lead. I've seen trucks stop quickly and, even though the dog was tied, it fell out and was dragged.

Another advantage of the crate is that it is a safe place to leave him if you need to run into the store. Otherwise you wouldn't be able to leave the windows down. Keep in mind that while many dogs are overly protective in their crates, this

may not be enough to deter dognappers. In some states it is against the law to leave a dog in the car unattended.

Before any car excursion be sure your puppy is allowed plenty of time outdoors to attend to his needs.

Crates are a safe way for your dog to travel. The fiberglass crates are the safest for air travel, but the metal crates allow for better air circulation.

Never leave a dog loose in the car wearing a collar and leash. More than one dog has killed himself by hanging. Do not let him put his head out an open window. Foreign debris can be blown into his eyes. When leaving your dog unattended in a car, consider the temperature. It can take less than five minutes to reach temperatures over 100 degrees Fahrenheit.

TRIPS

Perhaps you are taking a trip. Give consideration to what is best for your dog—traveling with you or boarding. When traveling by car, van or motor home, you need to think ahead about locking your vehicle. In all probability you have many valuables in the car and do not wish to leave it unlocked. Perhaps most valuable and not replaceable is your dog. Give thought to securing your vehicle and providing adequate ventilation for him. Another consideration for you when traveling with your dog is medical problems that may arise and little inconveniences, such as exposure to external parasites. Some areas of the country are quite flea infested. You may want to carry flea spray with you. This is even a good idea when staying in motels. Quite possibly you are not the only occupant of the room.

Unbelievably many motels and even hotels do allow canine guests, even some very first-class ones. Gaines Pet Foods Corporation publishes *Touring With Towser*, a directory of domestic hotels and motels that accommodate guests with dogs. Their address is Gaines TWT, PO Box 5700, Kankakee, IL, 60902. Call ahead to any motel that you may be considering and see if they accept pets. Sometimes it is necessary to pay a deposit against room damage. The management may feel reassured if you mention that your dog will be crated. If you do travel with your

If you decide to bring your German Shorthaired Pointers with you when you travel, bring along some familiar things to make them feel more at home.

Your puppy's well being is important to you, so be sure to inquire about airline and hotel regulations before making travel plans.

dog, take along plenty of baggies so that you can clean up after him. When we all do our share in cleaning up, we make it possible for motels to continue accepting our pets. As a matter of fact, you should practice cleaning up everywhere you take your dog.

Depending on where your are traveling, you may need an up-to-date health certificate issued by your veterinarian. It is good policy to take along your dog's medical information, which would include the name, address and phone number of your veterinarian, vaccination record, rabies certificate, and any medication he is taking.

AIR TRAVEL

When traveling by air, you need to contact the airlines to check their policy. Usually you have to make arrangements up to a couple of weeks in advance for traveling with your dog. The airlines require your dog to travel in an airline approved fiberglass crate. Usually these can be purchased through the airlines but they are also readily available in most pet-supply stores. If your dog is not accustomed to a crate, then it is a good idea to get him acclimated to it before your trip. The day of the actual trip you should withhold water about one hour ahead of departure and no food for about 12 hours. The airlines generally have temperature restrictions, which do not allow pets to travel if it is either too cold or too hot. Frequently these restrictions are based on the temperatures at the departure and arrival airports. It's best to inquire about a health certificate. These usually need to be issued within ten days of departure. You should arrange for non-stop, direct flights and if a commuter plane should be involved, check to see if it will carry dogs. Some don't. The Humane Society of the United States has put together a tip sheet for airline traveling. You can receive a copy by sending a self-addressed stamped envelope to:

The Humane Society of the United States
Tip Sheet
2100 L Street NW
Washington, DC 20037.

Regulations differ for traveling outside of the country and are sometimes changed without notice. Well in advance you need to write or call the appropriate consulate or agricultural department for instructions. Some countries have lengthy quarantines (six months), and countries differ in their rabies vaccination requirements. For instance, it may have to be given at least 30 days ahead of your departure.

Do make sure your dog is wearing proper identification including your name, phone number and city. You never know when you might be in an accident and separated from your

Make sure your GSP wears a collar with tags at all times. This will increase your chances of being reunited should you become separated.

dog. Or your dog could be frightened and somehow manage to escape and run away.

Another suggestion would be to carry in-case-of-emergency instructions. These would include the address and phone number of a relative or friend, your veterinarian's name, address and phone number, and your dog's medical information.

BOARDING KENNELS

Perhaps you have decided that you need to board your dog. Your veterinarian can recommend a good boarding facility or possibly a pet sitter that will come to your house.

The GSP is an accommodating dog and will make himself right at home wherever you go.

It is customary for the boarding kennel to ask for proof of vaccination for the DHLPP, rabies and bordetella vaccine. The bordetella should have been given within six months of boarding. This is for your protection. If they do not ask for this proof I would not board at their kennel. Ask about flea control. Those dogs that suffer flea-bite allergy can get in trouble at a boarding kennel. Unfortunately boarding kennels are limited on how much they are able to do.

For more information on pet sitting, contact NAPPS:
National Association of Professional Pet Sitters
1200 G Street, NW
Suite 760
Washington, DC 20005.

Some pet clinics have technicians that pet sit and technicians that board clinic patients in their homes. This may be an alternative for you. Ask your veterinarian if they have an employee that can help you. There is a definite advantage of having a technician care for your dog, especially if your dog is on medication or is a senior citizen.

You can write for a copy of *Traveling With Your Pet* from ASPCA, Education Department, 441 E. 92nd Street, New York, NY 10128.

IDENTIFICATION and Finding the Lost Dog

There are several ways of identifying your dog. The old standby is a collar with dog license, rabies, and ID tags. Unfortunately collars have a way of being separated from the dog and tags fall off. We're not suggesting you shouldn't use a collar and tags. If they stay intact and on the dog, they are the quickest way of identification.

For several years owners have been tattooing their dogs. Some tattoos use a number with a registry. Here lies the problem because there are several registries to check. If you wish to tattoo, use your social security number. The humane shelters have the means to trace it. It is usually done on the inside of the rear thigh. The area is first shaved and numbed. There is no pain, although a few dogs do not like the buzzing sound. Occasionally tattooing is not legible and needs to be redone.

Make sure you have a clear recent picture of your dog to distribute in case he becomes lost. Ch. Tabor's Laden Field Tuckoma. Owners, K. and C. Tucker.

The newest method of identification is microchipping. The microchip is a computer chip that is no larger than a grain of rice. The veterinarian implants it by injection between the shoulder blades. The dog feels no discomfort. If your dog is lost and picked up by the humane society, they can trace you by scanning the microchip, which has its own code. Microchip scanners are friendly to other brands of microchips and their registries. The microchip comes with a dog tag saying the dog is microchipped. It is the safest way of identifying your dog.

FINDING THE LOST DOG

I am sure you will agree that there would be little worse than losing your dog. Responsible pet owners rarely lose their dogs. They do not let their dogs run free because they don't want harm to come to them. Not only that but in most, if not all, states there is a leash law.

Beware of fenced-in yards. They can be a hazard. Dogs find ways to escape either over or under the fence. Another fast exit is through the gate that perhaps the neighbor's child left unlocked.

Below is a list that hopefully will be of help to you if you need it. Remember don't give up, keep looking. Your dog is worth your efforts.

1. Contact your neighbors and put flyers with a photo on it in their mailboxes. Information you should include would be the dog's name, breed, sex, color, age, source of identification, when your dog was last seen and where, and your name and phone numbers. It may be helpful to say the dog needs medical care. Offer a *reward*.

2. Check all local shelters daily. It is also possible for your dog to be picked up away from home and end up in an out-of-the-way shelter. Check these too. Go in person. It is not good enough to call. Most shelters are limited on the time they can hold dogs then they are put up for adoption or euthanized. There is the possibility that your dog will not make it to the shelter for several days. Your dog could have been wandering or someone may have tried to keep him.

3. Notify all local veterinarians. Call and send flyers.

4. Call your breeder. Frequently breeders are contacted when one of their breed is found.

5. Contact the rescue group for your breed.

6. Contact local schools—children may have seen your dog.

7. Post flyers at the schools, groceries, gas stations, convenience stores, veterinary clinics, groomers and any other place that will allow them.

8. Advertise in the newspaper.

9. Advertise on the radio.

BEHAVIOR and Canine Communication

Studies of the human/animal bond point out the importance of the unique relationships that exist between people and their pets. Those of us who share our lives with pets understand the special part they play through companionship, service and protection. For many, the pet/owner bond goes beyond simple companionship; pets are often considered members of the family. A leading pet food manufacturer recently conducted a nationwide survey of pet owners to gauge just how important pets were in their lives. Here's what they found:

· 76 percent allow their pets to sleep on their beds
· 78 percent think of their pets as their children
· 84 percent display photos of their pets, mostly in their homes
· 84 percent think that their pets react to their own emotions
· 100 percent talk to their pets
· 97 percent think that their pets understand what they're saying

Are you surprised?

Senior citizens show more concern for their own eating habits when they have the responsibility of feeding a dog. Seeing that their dog is routinely exercised encourages the owner to think of schedules that otherwise may seem

Children make great playmates for an energetic puppy and caring for him teaches a child responsibility and respect for animals.

unimportant to the senior citizen. The older owner may be arthritic and feeling poorly but with responsibility for his dog he has a reason to get up and get moving. It is a big plus if his dog is an attention seeker who will demand such from his owner.

Over the last couple of decades, it has been shown that pets relieve the stress of those who lead busy lives. Owning a pet has been known to lessen the occurrence of heart attack and stroke.

Many single folks thrive on the companionship of a dog. Lifestyles are very different from a long time ago, and today more individuals seek the single

It is important to keep in mind that your German Shorthaired Pointer wants to please you, and with patience will learn what you have to teach him.

Puppies possess innate curiosity and can "fall" into all sorts of predicaments. Be sure to supervise your pup at all times.

life. However, they receive fulfillment from owning a dog.

Most likely the majority of our dogs live in family environments. The companionship they provide is well worth the effort involved. In my opinion, every child should have the opportunity to have a family dog. Dogs teach responsibility through understanding their care, feelings and even respecting their life cycles. Frequently those children who have not been exposed to dogs grow up afraid of dogs, which isn't good. Dogs sense timidity and some will take advantage of the situation.

Today more dogs are serving as service dogs. Since the origination of the Seeing Eye dogs years ago, we now have trained hearing dogs. Also dogs are trained to provide service for the handicapped and are able to perform many different tasks for their owners. Search and Rescue dogs, with their handlers, are sent throughout the world to assist in recovery of disaster victims. They are life savers.

Today German Shorthaired Pointers can lead lives of service— as trained aide dogs or as man's best friend!

If you teach your German Shorthaired Pointer proper behavior as a puppy, he will be a model canine citizen in adulthood. FC/NAFC Markar's Radioactive. Owned by Mark Oakley.

Therapy dogs are very popular with nursing homes, and some hospitals even allow them to visit. The inhabitants truly look forward to their visits. They wanted and were allowed to have visiting dogs in their beds to hold and love.

Nationally there is a Pet Awareness Week to educate students and others about the value and basic care of our pets. Many countries take an even greater interest in their pets than Americans do. In those countries the pets are allowed to accompany their owners into restaurants and shops, etc. In the U.S. this freedom is only available to our service dogs. Even so we think very highly of the human/animal bond.

CANINE BEHAVIOR

Canine behavior problems are the number-one reason for pet owners to dispose of their dogs, either through new homes, humane shelters or euthanasia. Unfortunately there are too many owners who are unwilling to devote the necessary time to properly train their dogs. On the other hand, there are those who not only are concerned about inherited health problems but are also aware of the dog's mental stability.

You may realize that a breed and his group relatives (i.e., sporting, hounds, etc.) show tendencies to behavioral characteristics. An experienced breeder can acquaint you with his breed's personality. Unfortunately many breeds are labeled with poor temperaments when actually the breed as a whole is not affected but only a small percentage of individuals within the breed.

Children make great playmates for the energetic and patient German Shorthaired Pointer. Tabor's Roxanne of Zephyr will do anything for his young friend.

Inheritance and environment contribute to the dog's behavior. Some naïve people suggest inbreeding as the cause of bad temperaments. Inbreeding only results in poor behavior if the ancestors carry the trait. If there are excellent temperaments behind the dogs, then inbreeding will promote good temperaments in the offspring. Did you ever consider that inbreeding is what sets the characteristics of a breed? A purebred dog is the end result of inbreeding. This does not spare the mixed-breed dog from the same problems. Mixed-breed dogs frequently are the offspring of purebred dogs.

Not too many decades ago most of our dogs led a different lifestyle than what is prevalent today. Usually mom stayed home so the dog had human companionship and someone to discipline it if needed. Not much was expected from the dog. Today's mom works and everyone's life is at a much faster pace.

The dog may have to adjust to being a "weekend" dog. The family is gone all day during the week, and the dog is left to his own devices for entertainment. Some dogs sleep all day waiting for their family to come home and others become wigwam wreckers if given the opportunity. Crates do ensure the safety of the dog and the house. However, he could become a physically and

Although some traits are inherited within a breed, every GSP is an individual with his own personality.

emotionally cripple if he doesn't get enough exercise and attention. We still appreciate and want the companionship of our dogs although we expect more from them. In many cases we tend to forget dogs are just that—*dogs* not human beings.

SOCIALIZING AND TRAINING

Many prospective puppy buyers lack experience regarding the proper socialization and training needed to develop the type of pet we all desire. In the first 18 months, training does take some work. It is easier to start proper training before there is a problem that needs to be corrected.

Behavior and health problems can be passed down from generation to generation, so be sure to check your puppy's lineage very carefully.

The initial work begins with the breeder. The breeder should start socializing the puppy at five to six weeks of age and cannot let up. Human socializing is critical up through 12 weeks of age and likewise important during the following months. The litter should be left together during the first few weeks but it is necessary to separate them by ten weeks of age. Leaving them together after that time will increase competition for litter dominance. If puppies are not socialized with people by 12 weeks of age, they will be timid in later life.

The eight- to ten-week age period is a fearful time for puppies. They need to be handled very gently around children and adults. There should be no harsh discipline during this time. Starting at 14 weeks of age, the puppy begins the juvenile period, which ends when he reaches sexual maturity around six to 14 months of age. During the juvenile period he needs to be introduced to strangers (adults, children and other dogs) on the home property. At sexual maturity he will begin to bark at strangers and become more protective. Males start to lift their legs to urinate but if you desire you can inhibit this behavior by walking your boy on leash away from trees, shrubs, fences, etc.

With the proper supervision, your puppy should be allowed to experience and explore his surroundings.

Perhaps you are thinking about an older puppy. You need to inquire about the puppy's social experience. If he has lived in a kennel, he may have a hard time adjusting to people and environmental stimuli. Assuming he has had a good social upbringing, there are advantages to an older puppy.

Training includes puppy kindergarten and a minimum of one to two basic training classes. During these classes you will learn how to dominate your youngster. This is especially important if you own a large breed of dog. It is somewhat harder, if not nearly impossible, for some owners to be the Alpha figure when their dog towers over them. You will be taught how to properly restrain your dog. This concept is important. Again it puts you in the Alpha position. All dogs need to be restrained many times during their lives. Believe it or not, some of our worst offenders are the eight-week-old puppies that are brought to our clinic. They need to be gently

Puppies will find mischief whenever possible! You will have to play the role of pack leader in order to teach your German Shorthaired Pointer appropriate behavior.

restrained for a nail trim but the way they carry on you would think we were killing them. In comparison, their vaccination is a "piece of cake." When we ask dogs to do something that is not agreeable to them, then their worst comes out. Life will be easier for your dog if you expose him at a young age to the necessities of life—proper behavior and restraint.

UNDERSTANDING THE DOG'S LANGUAGE

Most authorities agree that the dog is a descendent of the wolf. The dog and wolf have similar traits. For instance both are pack oriented and prefer not to be isolated for long periods of time. Another characteristic is that the dog, like the wolf, looks to the leader—Alpha—for direction. Both the wolf and the dog communicate through body language, not only within their pack but with outsiders.

Every pack has an Alpha figure. The dog looks to you, or should look to you, to be that leader. If your dog doesn't receive the proper training and guidance, he very well may replace you as Alpha. This would be a serious problem and is certainly a disservice to your dog.

Eye contact is one way the Alpha wolf keeps order within his pack. You are Alpha so you must establish eye contact with your puppy. Obviously your puppy will have to look at you. Practice eye contact even if you need to hold his head for five to ten seconds at a time. You can give him a treat as a reward. Make sure your eye contact is gentle and not threatening. Later, if he has been naughty, it is permissible to give him a long, penetrating look. There are some older dogs that never learned eye contact as puppies and cannot accept eye contact. You should avoid eye contact with these dogs since they feel threatened and will retaliate as such.

BODY LANGUAGE

A lot can be learned about a puppy's behavior and attitude simply by observing his body language.

The play bow, when the forequarters are down and the hindquarters are elevated, is an invitation to play. Puppies play fight, which helps them learn the acceptable limits of biting. This is necessary for later in their lives. Nevertheless, an owner may

be falsely reassured by the playful nature of his dog's aggression. Playful aggression toward another dog or human may be an indication of serious aggression in the future. Owners should never play fight or play tug-of-war with any dog that is inclined to be dominant.

Signs of submission are:
1. Avoids eye contact.
2. Active submission—the dog crouches down, ears back and the tail is lowered.
3. Passive submission—the dog rolls on his side with his hindlegs in the air and frequently urinates.

Signs of dominance are:
1. Makes eye contact.
2. Stands with ears up, tail up and the hair raised on his neck.
3. Shows dominance over another dog by standing at right angles over it.

Dominant dogs tend to behave in characteristic ways such as:
1. The dog may be unwilling to move from his place (i.e., reluctant to give up the sofa if the owner wants to sit there).
2. He may not part with toys or objects in his mouth and may show possessiveness with his food bowl.
3. He may not respond quickly to commands.
4. He may be disagreeable for grooming and dislikes to be petted.

Dogs are a very important part of their owner's lives, and the bond between humans and animals is a strong one. These GSP elves get in on the Christmas fun.

Dogs are popular because of their sociable nature. Those that have contact with humans during the first 12 weeks of life regard them as a member of their own species—their pack. All dogs have the potential for both dominant and submissive behavior. Only through experience and training do they learn to whom it is appropriate to show which behavior. Not all dogs are concerned with dominance but owners need to be aware of that potential. It is wise for the owner to establish his dominance early on.

A human can express dominance or submission toward a dog in the following ways:
1. Meeting the dog's gaze signals dominance. Averting the gaze signals submission. If the dog growls or threatens, averting the gaze is the first avoiding action to take—it may prevent attack. It is important to establish eye contact in the puppy. The older dog that has not been exposed to eye contact may see it as a threat and will not be willing to submit.
2. Being taller than the dog signals dominance; being lower signals submission. This is why, when attempting to make friends with a strange dog or catch the runaway, one should kneel down to his level. Some owners see their

dogs become dominant when allowed on the furniture or on the bed. Then he is at the owner's level.

3. An owner can gain dominance by ignoring all the dog's social initiatives. The owner pays attention to the dog only when he obeys a command.

No dog should be allowed to achieve dominant status over any adult or child. Ways of preventing are as follows:

1. Handle the puppy gently, especially during the three- to four-month period.

2. Let the children and adults handfeed him and teach him to take food without lunging or grabbing.

3. Do not allow him to chase children or joggers.

4. Do not allow him to jump on people or mount their legs. Even females may be inclined to mount. It is not only a male habit.

Your puppy must be taught to behave. The result will be a well-mannered and amiable companion.

A puppy should not be forced into a situation he finds frightening. Respect his feelings and allow him time to acclimate to the situation.

5. Do not allow him to growl for any reason.
6. Don't participate in wrestling or tug-of-war games.
7. Don't physically punish puppies for aggressive behavior.

Restrain him from repeating the infraction and teach an alternative behavior. Dogs should earn everything they receive from their owners. This would include sitting to receive petting or treats, sitting before going out the door and sitting to receive the collar and leash. These types of exercises reinforce the owner's dominance.

Young children should never be left alone with a dog. It is important that children learn some basic obedience commands so they have some control over the dog. They will gain the respect of their dog.

FEAR

One of the most common problems dogs experience is being fearful. Some dogs are more afraid than others. On the lesser side, which is sometimes humorous to watch, dogs can be afraid of a strange object. They act silly when something is out of place in the house. We call his problem perceptive intelligence. He realizes the abnormal within his known environment. He does not react the same way in strange environments since he does not know what is normal.

On the more serious side is a fear of people. This can result in backing off, seeking his own space and saying "leave me alone" or it can result in an aggressive behavior that may lead to challenging the person. Respect that the dog wants to be left alone and give him time to come forward. If you approach the cornered dog, he may resort to snapping. If you leave him alone, he may decide to come forward, which should be rewarded with a treat.

Some dogs may initially be too fearful to take treats. In these cases it is helpful to make sure the dog hasn't eaten for about 24 hours. Being a little hungry encourages him to accept the treats, especially if they are of the "gourmet" variety.

Dogs can be afraid of numerous things, including loud noises and thunderstorms. Invariably the owner rewards (by comforting) the dog when it shows signs of fearfulness. When your dog is frightened, direct his attention to something else and act happy. Don't dwell on his fright.

AGGRESSION

Some different types of aggression are: predatory, defensive, dominance, possessive, protective, fear induced, noise provoked, "rage" syndrome (unprovoked aggression), maternal and aggression directed toward other dogs. Aggression is the most common behavioral problem encountered. Protective

Your German Shorthaired Pointer's relationship with other dogs is an essential one. This bunch of friends poses for a group portrait.

154

breeds are expected to be more aggressive than others but with the proper upbringing they can make very dependable companions. You need to be able to read your dog.

Many factors contribute to aggression including genetics and environment. An improper environment, which may include the living conditions, lack of social life, excessive punishment, being attacked or frightened

Puppies are particularly social creatures, they need the company of other puppies when young. The more people and animals he meets, the better socialized he will become.

GSPs just get better as the years pass! Sixteen-year-old Orion and twelve-year-old Ch Malhaven's Pride of Buck Hollow demonstrate the more mellow perks of owning an older dog.

by an aggressive dog, etc., can all influence a dog's behavior. Even spoiling him and giving too much praise may be detrimental. Isolation and the lack of human contact or

exposure to frequent teasing by children or adults also can ruin a good dog.

Lack of direction, fear, or confusion lead to aggression in those dogs that are so inclined. Any obedience exercise, even the sit and down, can direct the dog and overcome fear and/or confusion. Every dog should learn these commands as a youngster, and there should be periodic reinforcement.

When a dog is showing signs of aggression, you should speak calmly (no screaming or hysterics) and firmly give a command that he understands, such as the sit. As soon as your dog obeys, you have assumed your dominant position. Aggression presents a problem because there may be danger to others. Sometimes it is an emotional issue. Owners may consciously or unconsciously encourage their dog's aggression. Other owners show responsibility by accepting the problem and taking measures to keep it under control. The owner is responsible for his dog's actions, and it is not wise to take a chance on someone being bitten, especially a child. Euthanasia is the solution for some owners and in severe cases this may be the best

Although they may seem standoffish at times, GSP's are loving and affectionate pets.

These two German Shorthaired Pointers have clearly been well socialized. Tabor's Athena and Ch. Tabor's Artemis of Buck Hollow share a ball.

choice. However, few dogs are that dangerous and very few are that much of a threat to their owners. If caution is exercised and professional help is gained early on, most cases can be controlled.

Some authorities recommend feeding a lower protein (less than 20 percent) diet. They believe this can aid in reducing aggression. If the dog loses weight, then vegetable oil can be added. Veterinarians and behaviorists are having some success with pharmacology. In many cases treatment is possible and can improve the situation.

If you have done everything according to "the book" regarding training and socializing and are still having a behavior problem, don't procrastinate. It is important that the problem gets attention before it is out of hand. It is estimated that 20 percent of a veterinarian's time may be devoted to dealing with problems before they become so intolerable that the dog is separated from its home and owner. If your veterinarian isn't able to help, he should refer you to a behaviorist.

Punishment

A puppy should learn that correction is sometimes necessary and should not question your authority. An older dog that has never received correction may retaliate. In my opinion there will be a time for physical punishment but this does not mean hitting the dog. Do not use newspapers, fly swatters, etc. One type of correction, that is used by the mother dog when she corrects her puppies, is to take the puppy by the scruff and shake him *gently*. For the older, larger dog you can grab the scruff, one hand on each side of his neck, and lift his legs off the ground. This is effective since dogs feel intimidated when their feet are off the ground. Timing is of the utmost importance when punishment is necessary. Depending on the degree of fault, you might want to reinforce punishment by ignoring your dog for 15 to 20 minutes. Whatever you do, do not overdo corrections or they will lose value.

The most important advice to you is to be aware of your dog's actions. Even so, remember dogs are dogs and will behave as such even though we might like them to be perfect little people. You and your dog will become neurotic if you worry about every little indiscretion. When there is reason for concern—don't waste time. Seek guidance. Dogs are meant to be loved and enjoyed.

References:

Manual of Canine Behavior, Valerie O'Farrell, British Small Animal Veterinary Association.

Good Owners, Great Dogs, Brian Kilcommons, Warner Books.

Your German Shorthaired Pointer is happiest when being loved and enjoyed. Although correction will sometimes be necessary, it will all prove worthwhile in the end.

158

SUGGESTED READING

TS-214
Skin & Coat Care For Your Dog
432 pages, over 300 full-color photos

TS-249
Owner's Guide to Dog Health
224 pages, over 190 full-color photos

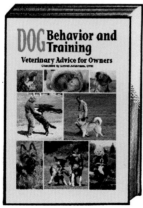

TS-252
Dog Behavior and Training
292 pages, over 200 full-color photos

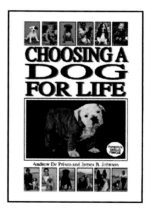

TS-257
Choosing A Dog for Life
384 pages, over 700 full-color photos

INDEX